Trading Chaos

WILEY FINANCE EDITIONS

Trading Chaos

❖

Applying Expert Techniques to
Maximize Your Profits

BILL WILLIAMS

John Wiley & Sons, Inc.
New York • Chichester • Brisbane • Toronto • Singapore

Bill M. Williams, Ph.D., is a registered Commodity Trading Advisor with the Commodity Futures Trading Commission and is a member of the National Futures Association. As such he is required by law to include the following statement with any publication.

Please note that the above statement refers primarily to simulated trading programs that are designed with the benefit of hindsight. Profitunity Trading Group and Bill M. Williams, Ph.D. trade selection processes are made *before the fact* and have never been published with the benefit of hindsight. In addition PTG and Bill M. Williams make every possible effort to illustrate in text and performance records, any stop loss order that may have been gapped due to unusual market conditions.

This text is printed on acid-free paper.

Copyright © 1995 by Marketplace Books, Inc.
Published by John Wiley & Sons, Inc.

Library of Congress Cataloging-in-Publication Data:

Williams, Bill, 1932–
    Trading Chaos : applying expert techniques to maximize your profits / Bill Williams.
      p. cm. — (Wiley finance editions)
    ISBN 0-471-11929-6
    1. Capital market—Mathematical models. 2. Futures market—
Mathematical models. 3. Fractals. 4. Chaotic behavior in systems.
    I. Title. II. Series.
    HG4523.W554   1995
    332.64'5—dc20   95-2730

Printed in the United States of America
10 9 8 7 6 5 4 3

This book is dedicated to my loving partner, Ellen. She urged me to write it, helped shape it, and co-learned with me. Without her encouragement, I would have quit trading long before it became so profitable. Without her, I would have given up and sought a "real job" instead of enjoying the rewarding lifestyle of an independent speculator. Without her, this book would not exist. Thank you for being there for me, Ellen!

Preface

Unless we change our direction, we are most likely to end up where we are headed.

Chinese Proverb

The brutal truth is that 90 percent of all traders lose money consistently. About 5–7 percent tend to break even and only 3–5 percent actually make money regularly. This truth becomes even more astounding alongside two other factors: (1) traders, as a group, tend to fall in the top tenth percentile on intelligence quotient (IQ) tests and (2) the vast majority of this group of highly intelligent women and men have already been successful in professional and/or business pursuits before coming to trading.

Chances are overwhelming that you too are in the top intelligence group and have had significant success in your life. Otherwise, you would not be reading this preface. You may have already tried trading and know how difficult it is, or you may be thinking about going into trading for the first time. Either way, if you can solve the puzzle of why nine out of ten of this elite, well-endowed group lose money consistently, you will discover unlimited profit potential for yourself.

The immediate question is: Are you ready and willing to give up the artificiality of tiresome technical analysis and learn instead what is more "natural"?

This book will show you a simple and precise way to solve this puzzle so that you can be among the consistent winners rather than the chronic losers. How can I be so sure? Because I have conducted trader training seminars for over 20,000 traders and have privately trained over 450 people who are now full-time traders. I am a trader with over 35 years of successful experience in the markets. The material in this book comes primarily from my private tutorials.

The first thing you must *not* do is act like the 90 percent majority, who are chronic losers. Losers spend too much time reading *The Wall Street Journal,* listening to CNBC-FNN, reading books on technical and fundamental analyses, calling their brokers, attending smorgasbord seminars, buying systems, and subscribing to newsletters and hotlines. They spend most of their trading lives riding on a wild, nonstop merry-go-round that keeps them busy and takes them nowhere.

My approach is different. This book will show you an updated map and a new and better way to realize consistent profits using the latest scientific theories of human and economic behavior. This new approach is derived from the science of *chaos.* I call it the "Profitunity" approach.

Chaos gives us new lenses through which to view the market. It enables us to see the underlying structure that controls market behavior. It also takes the ambiguity out of Elliot wave counting.

While chaos (a very bad misnomer, which we will address in Chapter 3) is older than civilization itself, it became a practical tool only after powerful computers became available.

You don't need powerful computers for this type of trading. The giant computers (super mainframes) were necessary initially to extricate the important underlying structural and behavioral aspects of the markets, which completely elude average traders.

Fractal geometry, a division of the science of chaos, provides a technique that will let you analyze any market and know exactly what to do in 10 seconds or less. Most of my students are experienced traders who formerly spent decades of 6- to 10-hour days doing technical analysis.

Until recently, most traders and scientists ignored or denied this quirky and forbidding side of nature. They preferred studying Newton's reassuring machines or the planets' smooth elliptical orbits. Although these "ideal" models are now known to be aberrations of nature, it's easy to understand their appeal. Classical physics follows a smooth, uninterrupted path.

Chaotic (natural) systems are not so obliging: *nonlinear dynamics* are at work. Such phenomena are sustained by complex loops of feedback into the system at unpredictable points in its cycle. For example, one pendulum swings to and fro with a regular back-and-forth motion, but if it is struck by the ball of a second pendulum before reaching its zenith, both pendulums may begin swinging in wildly erratic patterns. Similarly, when an ocean breaker bounces off a jetty, it collides with oncoming waves that variously enhance or diminish its size. In the human brain, the electrical impulse of one neuron gets unpredictably amplified or dampened by inputs it receives from connected neurons.

In the financial markets, a trend is enhanced or undermined by surprises in governmental announcements, weather patterns, crop reports, or political or economic actions by one or more influential nations. Such "kickbacks" send an apparently chaotic system flying off in a new direction that cannot be effectively charted using linear Newtonian tools.

This diversion seems to create a totally chaotic world. But, to the utter dismay of scientists, the unruly disorder everyone feared does not come. What begins as a mad jumble of impulses (price movement in the markets) eventually assumes a form—a ghostly geometry called a "strange attractor."

What exactly is a "strange attractor," and how can a predictable structure emerge from seeming disorder? Think of it as an idealized state toward which an unpredictable—that is, strange—system is attracted. That structure stems from the fact that the behavior of the system (market) is not totally random. Rather, the system vacillates erratically within a particular range or norm.

These insights lead to a friendlier view of chaos. What was once shunned by classical physicists as a terrifying mess has come to be embraced as a "higher form of order."

As Plato prophesied, "Geometry will show the soul toward the truth."

When charts of market action are transformed into an abstract structure (a strange attractor), one can immediately see the underlying behavior of the market. The difference is similar to viewing a broken bone with one's eyes versus seeing it with an X ray. The visual examination may indicate that something is amiss, but the X ray allows accurate assessment of exactly what is taking place in the underlying bone structure. What does this all mean? Understanding chaotic activity will be a tremendous asset in taking profits from the markets.

As you progress through the Profitunity approaches, you will learn why successful trading gets you dancing with the market, not wrestling with it. I spent 25 years fighting the markets, with profitable but inconsistent results; then fractal geometry proved that the markets are a natural function rather than a man-made function.

By understanding and using this approach, you remove most of the stress of trading. Your understanding gives you more control over what is happening between you and the market. And, just like dancing, if you are not having fun trading, you are doing it all wrong.

You will find in this book a simple, ascending path to trading success. A five-step progression from novice to expert will enable you to locate yourself precisely on this path: you will know not only where you are but exactly what you must do to progress to the next higher level.

You will find a new lifestyle opening up, where you make the rules and you determine your own future with a minimum of outside hassles and governmental regulations. You'll be free of the usual impediments of bosses, dissatisfied customers, returns, warehousing, financing, collecting, reports, staff meetings, FICA, sales tax, rent, depreciation, OSHA regulations, business licenses, and so on. Most people can only dream about a lifestyle like that.

All this will be possible because you will understand what the elite group—the top 10 percent—of traders know:

The markets are a natural function and their activity does not follow classical physics, parametric statistics, or linear math.

Fractal geometry offers an entirely different point of view with a different way of processing information, a way that can bring you consistent profits and an enviable lifestyle.

Another conclusion comes from the insights provided by the science of chaos: no one trades the markets; we all trade our own personal belief systems.

Because your belief systems come from your own twin-hemisphere neck-top computer, we will spend time, later in the book, getting your three-pound bundle of wetware into harmony with the market. When that harmony is driving your decisions, *winning becomes the path of least resistance.*

Paul Rapp, a world-recognized brain scientist, states that, "If there is a Holy Grail to neural functioning, chaos theory will help to find it." I am sure that the same prediction applies to market behavior.

This book gives you what I know to be true in trading the markets. How much might it be worth to you? Neither you nor I can determine an amount in advance. However, I can assure you that hundreds of other people, using this material, have changed not only their trading results but their entire lives as well. There is an old Southern saying:

Anyone can count the seeds in an apple.

No one can count the apples in a seed.

Let me welcome you to the wonderfully enlightening, informative, profitable, and entertaining journey of becoming an *expert trader.*

BILL WILLIAMS

Mobile, Alabama
April 1995

Acknowledgments

Many friends and colleagues fed me at my learning trough. I wish to acknowledge particularly: Dr. Ida Rolf, who traded soybeans at night while she taught me about the body during the day; Larry Williams, who motivated me to try trading futures instead of stocks and who was responsible for getting me on CNBC-FNN; Tim Slater, who sent me around the world to share my research and information with other traders; Tom Joseph, who is one of the world's best researchers and sharers; Bill Cruz and Darla Tuttle of Omega Research, for making our research easily available on Trade Station; Rick Knox and Commodity Quote Graphics, for their unwavering support over many years of trying new ideas and making their expertise and equipment available; Joel Robbins, who first published our research; Rick Boerke, Mike Boren, and Chris Kamberis, three of the best brokers in the world, who saw us through our great successes and our not-so-great failures; at John Wiley & Sons, Chris Myers and Myles Thompson made this book possible and took the financial risks involved in publishing it; Jacqueline Urinyi, my editor; Maryan Malone of Publications Development Company, who made it more *readable*; and others too numerous to mention. Equally important are all the 450-plus individual traders who have attended our private tutorials, proving, beyond any doubt, that profitable trading can be taught.

Contents

1

A Look at the Current Reality of Trading

The beginning is the most important part of the work.

Plato

GOAL: TO UNDERSTAND THE AVERAGE TRADER'S VIEW AND EXPERIENCE OF THE MARKET

The market is not your problem. Your problem is that you *see* the market as your problem.

Once upon a time, people got together, swapped things, and traded. The trading of goods wasn't something they analyzed or fussed and fretted over; it was just something they did along with planting seeds in the spring, harvesting crops in the fall, and then trading with their neighbors for wild game, tools, or other necessities. If they had a trading problem, they sought advice from their parents and grandparents, great uncles, older brothers, and other people who were successful traders. In the past, these were the experts, and the practical advice they gave was based on real-life experiences.

Then came the sophistication of the second half of the 20th century. After World War II, there arose an entirely different class of traders: trading experts—the ones with degrees, great

1

mahogany desks, and polished nameplates on their doors. Before long, rhetoric replaced reality as the primary shaper of trading practices. Nonsense replaced common sense. Our interest became centered around moving averages, stochastics, RSI, point and figures, oscillators, dmi, adx, cci, volatility, bullish consensus, momentum, roc, MACD, plus numerous other indicators. Then came the newsletters and books such as *How I Made 40 Million Last Year Trading One Eurodollar Contract.* In the early 1980s, a flurry of $3,000 black box systems sold at incredible rates. None proved profitable and all have been discarded.

Market profile hit the scene but was hampered because it used parametric statistics in a nonparametric world (the market). When the statistics proved useless, we looked back thousands of years and borrowed candlestick analysis from the Japanese. If they endured, they must be effective, right?

Now, we are in the midst of a psychological revolution for traders that features everything from psychobabble, subliminal messages, and hypnosis to NLP, usually taught in groups by nontraders or traders who will not trade while outsiders are watching.

Not surprisingly, aspiring traders become confused, disappointed, and baffled, and lose control of themselves. The vast majority of them join the ranks of the chronic losers.

Over the past 20 years, we have taken a practical and commonsense job of trading, dressed it in fancy language, and turned it into something very abstract and difficult. What the experts haven't romanticized, sentimentalized, and idealized, they have scrutinized and analyzed to such an extent that we no longer are able to see the forest. We're too obsessed with the trees. The process of trading—or speculation, as it is now called—has been transformed into a pseudointellectual science; traders think they must strain their brains at it, in order to profit. Trading, however, is anything but an intellectual endeavor. In fact, the more you brain-strain, the more likely you are to find yourself with a losing P & L statement. There is ample evidence that the smarter you consciously try to be, the more difficult it will be for you to make a profit in trading. (We will examine this concept in detail in Chapter 12.)

Good trading does not emanate primarily from the head; it comes from the gut and the heart. Rather than long hard thought, you will need intuition and sensitivity to your needs and the needs of the market, and a firm grounding in the soil of common sense.

Traders who think too much tend to say things like "Trading is the hardest thing I've ever done." When they stop thinking so much about it, stop obsessing over all the little details, stop worrying about whether one decision will ruin their trading for life, and start paying at least as much attention to their own internal operations as to the needs of the market—that's when trading becomes a relatively easy, low-stress way to earn a good living.

Because I have traded actively for over 35 years and have held trading workshops in 12 countries on 5 continents, I am sometimes labeled as an expert. It's an accurate label. I am an expert at trading my own account. I have become an expert trader through trial and error, which is the only way anyone ever becomes an expert trader. I am not an expert as a result of having obtained a degree in engineering and a doctorate in psychology. My formal schooling actually did more to hinder my ability to trade than to help it. Graduate school filled my head with a lot of abstractions and theory about human behavior, but did nothing toward advancing my common sense. It caused me to think a lot about the "right way" to trade, and the harder I thought, the more I lost touch with my intuitive knowledge.

Trading is not so fundamentally difficult, but when the self-appointed gurus make it sound difficult, we make the mistake of believing them. They may have batches of degrees, but their rhetoric often conceals more than it reveals. Strip away their elegant intellectual language and you will discover some basic timeless truths that serve to make trading quite simple. The problem with these truths is that they are neither romantic nor sentimental. They are realistic, pragmatic, and hard-headed.

This book is all about returning to a commonsense vision of trading. Successful trading builds on knowledge of (1) the underlying structure of the market and (2) your own underlying structure. The way your brain works makes you a winner or a loser. The old advice, "Know yourself first and then know the market," has stood the test of time. We misplace our "common (trading) sense" when we try to make a technological science out of dealing with our own emotions.

When I first started full-time trading, I spent over $6,000 on subscriptions to newsletters. My actual cost was many times that amount, because I believed what these so-called experts were circulating. Then I did a little research and found out that these newsletter authors did not trade on their own recommendations. I was paying them substantial fees and risking my own hard-earned dollars, and they were unwilling to rely on their own analysis! Have you heard the argument: "I would lose my objectivity if I had my own money in there"? I call it B.S. excuse # 17.

Trading does not have to be difficult, and it can be very rewarding. Learn to depend on yourself in trading. You may not know it but you are an expert too, just like me. As you go through this book and learn the Profitunity approach to trading, you will begin to *enjoy being* a trader instead of worrying about *becoming* a trader.

WHAT ANIMAL MOST TYPIFIES THE MARKET TO YOU?

Before you read another sentence, please pause and answer this question: If the market were an animal, what animal

4

would it be? In other words, what animal best captures for you the characteristics of the market? Take a quick mental trip through the zoo and then write your answer in the space below.

To me, the market is a(n) _____.
(name of animal)

I'm asking you to actually write your answer because I want you to *make the decision*, have a written statement of your choice (no second thoughts, no looking back), and then have a concept of the market that you can visualize as we discuss it.

Now that you have conceptualized the market as your choice of an animal, I'll anticipate some of your questions:

1. What else is different about this approach?

A good question that deserves a serious answer. Let me suggest an experiment that you can do for yourself. Contact everyone you know who has traded commodities and quit for some reason (usually, couldn't win financially). Ask them why they quit—in other words, what prevented them from making a profit? I know what they will tell you: "I couldn't make money because I couldn't predict the market."

Know something? *No one can!* No one in the whole world knows what the bonds will do tomorrow. If you think you can learn to predict the market accurately, you'll take yourself out of the 10 percent who are successful financially.

This approach, using fractal analysis, is not primarily concerned with long-range prediction. Comedian Flip Wilson used to describe his "Church of What's Happening Now." Fractals are the market's equivalent of the Church of What's Happening Now. Fractal analysis gives a much clearer and more accurate picture of current market activity. In the Profitunity approach, we don't deal the deck; we just play the percentages.

While everyone else is using technical and fundamental analysis, we aren't. All technical analysis is built on the faulty premise that the future will be like the past. If there is one thing I have learned in over 35 years of trading, it is that the future will *not* be like the past.

In the 1960s and early 1970s, traders made fortunes trading beans on a ten-period moving average. Try that today and see how long you last.

2. What's the secret behind success with the Profitunity approach?

The best kept secret in the trading world: Almost nothing turns out as expected. The best trading plans usually go wrong. Notice that I didn't say sometimes, or occasionally; I said *usually*.

Most traders never discover this secret; it is not what they want to hear. Losing traders search for certainty and reliability. They want a system, an adviser, a hotline, or a market indicator they can count on to tell them what to do. And the less certainty they get from these props, the more they search for it.

SOME UNPOPULAR TRUTHS:
A TYPICAL SCENARIO

Most traders' lives are filled with a continuing series of starts that don't lead to happy endings. The vast majority of traders take daily doses of hope. They're sure that success is just around the corner.

Let's look at a typical trader's story and see how close it might come to your personal experience. If you haven't traded before, let me assure you that the odds are greatly in favor of this being your experience if you start trading and use technical and fundamental analysis.

You are attracted to the futures markets by the thought of "making a lot of money fast without having to work for it." Your initial interest is most likely aroused by knowing or hearing of someone who has made a great deal of money in futures. Your friend or personal acquaintance—or broker—will, from time to time, mention trades that yielded a nice profit. You'll never hear about the losses.

When you ask for details, your friend will tell about trading in gold or currencies—whatever is hot at the time. "This system works" will be the confident summary.

Next, becoming a little more talkative, your friend tells you about more successful trades: one deal made 70 percent on margin in four days, another brought a big gain in selling gold short over the weekend. Your friend sounds so confident, assured, and successful that you figure you are hearing the absolute truth and nothing but the truth.

Finally, you can't stand it anymore. You're hungry for that kind of success, so you garner the courage to ask whether you can shadow the next few trades. Your friend agrees to let you in on the next few trades, and you begin dreaming of how rich you will be soon.

Your first trade shows a small profit. The second one, a bean option that doubles in six weeks, does even better. Your dream of being rich is coming to life in your bank account. Maybe it's time to call Kansas for a Lear Jet catalog.

The next trade is a disaster, followed by another loser. You postpone your dream for a while.

When you ask your trading-genius friend what's happening, you are told, "It's just a brief slump—those things happen from time to time." Unfortunately, the losing streak continues, and finally you have to throw in the towel before your spouse gives you hell.

Your friend the expert, however, goes on trading and somehow still lives as well as ever.

Now, even though you have suffered losses, you've also tasted success. You know it is *possible* to make big profits; it just isn't easy.

Next, you subscribe to trading newsletters, you read brokerage reports, and you watch financial programs on TV. You find yourself thinking about trading all the time, even when you should be thinking about something else. You have a bad case of the possibilities.

You trade a little on your own, not telling your friend. You do better than you did as your friend's shadow, but you know you have a lot to learn. So you are receptive when a brochure comes in the mail about a trading seminar that will answer all your questions and make you the "trader of the month." Glowing recommendations from former attendees are quoted on every page. There will be a number of speakers, so there should be something for everyone. You sign up for the seminar.

One speaker shows you how to identify major turning points in the markets. She flashes charts of how she made money in the '87 crash and then followed up with a perfect call on the '89 crash. Her track record is incredible.

Another speaker, an Elliott wave specialist, promises an upcoming once-in-a-lifetime opportunity. If you want precise timing, you need to subscribe to his newsletter, fax line, and intraday telephone update. This costs quite a bit of money, but what the heck, you're going to be so rich it won't matter. You think of all the profits he has made, and of how he is such a nice guy to share all this wealth-building information with you.

It is so comforting to finally be working with a professional, someone quoted in *The Wall Street Journal* and *Futures* magazine. This is a *real* trader with a proven, documented track record. It doesn't hurt that he has a Rolex watch and is wearing an Armani suit.

You subscribe, and the newsletter says buy this and sell that. Some of the trades you just don't understand—they don't jibe with what was said in the seminar—but you make them

8

anyway because you don't want to lose out on any profits. Many of the trades work out quite nicely—well enough to offset the losers to sustain your confidence in the seminar–newsletter guru.

Then the big day arrives. The fax line shouts:

This is it—the big one!

The lead-in is irresistible: "This is our last chance. This is like buying gold at \$35 or stocks at 800. Sell the kids and mortgage the farm. Commit everything you have—and do it now!" Or words to that effect.

You are nervous but you know you must be bold to make big profits. You sell other investments you own, get a home equity loan from the bank, and buy in before it's too late. But the price goes down, not up.

You call your trading guru for comfort and advice and he says, "Wonderful! Just what we were hoping for—an opportunity to buy more at bargain prices."

Your collar's already too tight. You've invested all you can afford and then some.

The price continues downward and you need some money. You sell your futures contracts to pay off the loan. Depression sets in as you wonder what to do with the little money that's left.

You think that maybe you misunderstood the adviser's instruction. He is a registered Commodity Trading Adviser so he ought to know what he is doing. His newsletter continues to talk about how much money his clients are making. Possibly you bought in at a level that was too sophisticated and you need a more basic adviser. You are too nervous to stay with the strategy of the seminar and newsletter.

You read more books, including one called *Market Wizards* and another on *The New Market Wizards*. A couple of the stories point out that traders lose money when they trade without a system, when they jump from one trade to another without a careful plan for buying and selling.

That must be the problem! So you find a system that has been used for over 15 years and has produced an average annual profit of above 30 percent per year. You *know* you can't go wrong with a system like that.

Well, you do! Just as you begin using it, somehow it suffers its first losing year. Still, you keep on trading. You know that millions of dollars are made in the futures markets every day, and you only want a few of them.

You hear about spreads, where supposedly there is still great profit potential but more limited risk. You are older and wiser now, so you decide to take less risk and be more certain.

You are now very selective, employing only systems with documented track records. You join Club 3000 to commiserate with other mostly naive and consistent losers.

THE SEESAW

You've become more careful and consistent with your trading. The only problem is that you're not making money consistently; you're on a seesaw of losing and winning. The only consistent part of your trading is the percentage you spend on commissions.

Your scenario has made you decide that track records, research, and indicators are mostly shams. There is no way to separate the good from the bad advisers nor the honest from the dishonest. You're sure that there must be more crooks in this business per square foot than there are in the Mafia. You are just about resigned that you are not cut out to be a trader.

Still, you have to put your savings somewhere, and you want more than passbook or CD interest. You decide to go into a trading pool, where there seems to be less risk—and maybe more competent advisers. You choose a pool that has been very reliable through a series of winning years with little drawdown.

Newsletters and trading advisers may fudge their records, but pools are better regulated.

Unfortunately, the economy turns weak, the market sags, and the pool suffers a setback. It has its first losing year in the last ten.

You are recalled to active duty as a trader. You decide—again—that no one else riding the seesaw will look after your money the way you will. And on and on it goes. You don't even think about the call you might have made to Kansas.

THE WORLD OF TRADING

At every step, you've been careful to plan meticulously, to listen to only the best forecasters, to work with only proven systems, to employ the best and brightest minds—in short, to use only the best laid plans. Still, for some reason, nothing works out as it's supposed to. Welcome to the wonderful world of futures trading, where almost nothing turns out as expected. You are flooded with forecasts for the economy, for interest rates, for gold, for foreign currencies, but rarely does any forecast turn out to be accurate.

Newsletter writers boast of sensational track records, even though only a few of their readers renew their subscriptions.

Economists and advisers appear on FNN and at seminars to explain sensibly and convincingly why some event is inevitable. But the event never comes to pass or it occurs much later than anticipated.

Despite the plausible ideas, the computer-tested systems, the economic wisdom, the refined techniques, the documented track records, and the commonsense approaches, practically nothing in the economic or trading world works out as everyone was assured it would.

Some traders do make money over time. Actually, some traders do quite well consistently, over long periods of time. Those profits are made in spite of events that don't unfold as

11

promised. If you doubt this last statement, simply dig out last year's forecast issues of various newsletters. Read what the writer predicted was going to happen this year. Ask yourself how valuable those forecasts were. Make sure you read the original: the review and retelling may differ considerably.

Remember how H. Ross Perot, during the 1992 Presidential campaign, "guaranteed" us that there would be a catastrophic bank failure and we would see the demise of the FDIC during mid-December 1992?

Tune in to tonight's news analysis. Experts rarely agree on the significance of what's happening in the present, much less in the future.

The professional analysts-predictors strike an "I knew it was going to happen" stance because they feel it is necessary in their business. Each feels he or she must be in command of the situation, on top of the markets, aware of what is happening and what is going to happen. After all, their competitors are putting up the same false front.

Traders have their own reasons for keeping the real results secret. They risk their self-esteem along with their money when they trade. They don't want to appear to be the only losers when everyone else seems to be doing so well.

Most traders go on expecting the future to evolve predictably; they are positive that there's a reliable system and that other people have found it. They keep searching for a financial Rosetta Stone, but they never find it.

No one can tell when bonds will peak or how far they will fall. Human traders aren't able to predict the future in any reliable way. For every example of an investment forecast that came true, I can point to four or five that didn't—and some of both kinds may have come from the same forecaster.

When you give up the hope that some adviser, some system, some source of inside tips is going to give you a shortcut to wealth, you'll finally begin to gain control over your trading future. It will finally dawn on you that no one trades the market. Not you, not the "experts," not the technoids, not those institutions with three-story computers, no one. We all trade our own personal belief systems. When you recognize this truth, a whole new trading world opens up.

Trading is a psychological game. Economic, fundamental, mechanical, or technical strategies mostly don't work. As I write this, a recent issue of *Futures* magazine reports that, out of 231 professionally managed funds, only 33 are showing a gain about halfway through the calendar year. Only 3 out of 231, or just over 1 percent, are showing gains of more than 10 percent.[1] That translates to 87 percent losers and only 1 percent up more than 10 percent for the year. Remember, these are the results for the highest paid *professionals* managing some of the largest public funds in the world.

These traders have the biggest computers and the best information in the world available to them. But the markets are not computers and they cannot be understood by computers. There is an easy way to know exactly when computers will become successful as traders: as soon as they can tell the difference between a cat and a dog.

Trading the markets offers fantastic opportunities for making profits but it is at the same time the most self-revealing career anyone can choose.

We learn that understanding ourselves is the key to profit-making decisions and strategies. We see that, beyond the monetary results, there are rewards inherent in the activity of trading. A total approach for understanding the market requires strategy and tactics that let us understand ourselves as well as the markets.

We learn that the underlying structure of the market is a mirror of the underlying structure in each individual trader. The challenge is to harmonize our own individual underlying (and usually unseen) structure with that of the market.

[1] *Futures*, June 1994, p. 22.

Our search for success might be compared to the quest for the holy grail: we're looking for that one idea that will *guarantee* that we can be consistent winners. I propose that our quest can be summed up in five words: *Want what the market wants.* That goal is very simple but not always easy.

All of our frustrations and losses come from one source. We had expectations that were not met. When we want what the market wants, we have no frustrations. By aligning our own underlying structure with that of the market, we have no unfulfilled expectations.

With this approach, trading is a low-stress way to live. We learn that we can get into a psychological "no-risk" structure and have fun. We realize that if trading is not fun, we are doing something wrong, and the market, which is our only teacher, will always *always* tell us exactly what is wrong and where our errors lie.

FINDING YOUR NATURAL TRADING SELF

In this book, I will show you how you can find more safety and profit in the uncertain world of trading—without needing the right forecaster or system, without taking risks you shouldn't be taking, without getting upset, and without having to watch FNN or eat *The Wall Street Journal* for breakfast.

I cannot *guarantee* that you will equal my own trading success or even that you will make a profit using these ideas. Having privately trained over 450 people who are now full-time traders, I believe I can help you get the maximum return from your talent, your ambition, and your interest in trading.

Following the Profitunity approach will make your trading life easier and more enjoyable. You'll be able to discard your trading worries and you won't be taking on new pressures and concerns.

Because the market is unpredictable, we must approach trading with a method that does not demand predictability.

14

We don't need fortune-tellers, soothsayers, hotlines, or newsletters to guide us in our daily living because we understand that living is not predictable. You don't know what you will be thinking at this time next week. Neither can anyone really know what the markets will be thinking at this time next week.

We all trade our own belief systems. That's what Profitunity is all about. When we discover the underlying structure of the market and then align our personal underlying structure with that of the market, the result is geometric harmony.

The markets are characterized by energy. And energy always follows the path of least resistance. Think of a river flowing down a mountain. It follows the riverbed because that is the path of least resistance. Its movements and patterns (roaring or calm; the directions it takes) depend on the underlying structure of the riverbed. Most approaches to trading try to redirect the flow of the water instead of dealing with the underlying structure—the riverbed. The underlying structure of the futures market is the "fractal," which is best discovered by using the science of chaos.

Think of how, in your own life, you follow the path of least resistance. Following that path has led you to reading this page at this particular instant. From my many years as a psychologist, I realized that most psychotherapy does little or no good because it deals with behavior rather than the underlying structure that causes and directs that behavior.

If you deal with the underlying structure—change the riverbed—you will change the behavior of the river. How you use your brain in your trading is no different. The only two areas to master in trading are: (1) understanding the market and (2) understanding yourself. In this book, you will learn to do both, to understand the underlying structure of the market and of yourself. For example, you will learn that one indicator of this underlying structure happens 99.5 percent of the time when the market has a *significant high or low* (plus or minus one bar on the graph scales). I will prove to you that you can trust this indicator.

You will learn how you may be sabotaging yourself when you are trading. As you master the Profitunity approach, you will gain insight into your own behavior. That feature alone is worth many times the cost of this book.

Finally, we will integrate the Profitunity techniques so that, with a bit of practice, you can analyze any chart and know, in *10 seconds or less*, where you should be long, short, pyramiding, stopping and reversing, or just plain out of the market.

HOW THIS BOOK IS ORGANIZED

In this chapter, we have examined the frustrations and experiences of more than 90 percent of all traders. The markets, like human behavior, are inherently unpredictable. Our real quest is wanting what the market wants. The market, like everything else in the universe, always follows the path of least resistance.

In the next chapter, we will see just how simple the markets really are.

In Chapter 3, we examine in detail how the new logic from the science of chaos gives us a better map for trading.

Chapter 4 examines the key to *behavior*, the underlying and usually unseen structure. We will look at this underlying "structure of structure" in the market and how it affects your trading.

Chapter 5 includes a map for moving from being a novice trader to being an expert trader. You'll learn what indicators will tell you the level at which you are trading at the moment and what tools to use at each level.

Chapter 6 maps out the requirements for joining the top 10 percent of all traders. The purpose of the novice trader level is to *not* lose money while gaining experience in the market. The tools needed at this level are the "single bar analysis," volume, trend, reaction to new volume (the Market Facilitation Index, or MFI), the four Profitunity windows, and the Profitunity air bag that protects against wildly erratic markets.

Chapter 7 moves up one step. At this level, a trader is able to take money from the market consistently on a one-contract basis. The tool addressed in this chapter is the Elliott wave. Using the Profitunity MACD (moving average convergence divergence), we will take the ambiguity out of counting the waves so that you know where the market is and where it most likely will go next. At this point, you enter the top 3 percent of all traders.

Chapter 8 addresses the use of fractals and leverage. It permits trading the underlying structure of the Elliott wave, which enables you to trade inside the Elliott wave even when you are not sure which wave you are in. It also enables you to trade more successfully in both trending and range-bound markets.

Chapter 9 moves you up to the Competent level. Your purpose here is to maximize your return on investment (ROI) by varying your trading volume. You should be able to double whatever percentage return you are able to achieve at Level Two. The Profitunity Planned Trading™ tool allows the market itself to determine your optimum asset allocation tactics.

Chapter 10 ties the first nine chapters into a tidy 10-second analysis package. You will learn a simple checklist that ensures that you are considering all the relevant information before making an executive decision on when and how to trade. The tool that permits this is the Profitunity Trading Partner.™ You then enter the top 2 percent of all traders.

Chapter 11 brings in an entirely new perspective and focus. Chapters 6 through 10 examine and use the underlying structure of the market. Chapter 11 examines and begins to use your own personal underlying structure, bringing you to Level Four. We examine first your own unique hardware (your body structure and how that influences the way you perceive the markets and the world). Next, we take an intensive look at the human brain "wiring," to understand and control which of the three "traders" inside the body might be running the show at a particular moment. When you put these factors together with the underlying structure of the market, winning becomes the path of least resistance.

Chapter 12 brings you to the pinnacle of trading, where our primary reason for trading is to "find out who we are." You will learn how to put trading into a psychological "no-risk" situation that makes trading a low-stress, fun way to live.

YOUR MARKET ANIMAL

I have had a lifelong interest in physics and have read several biographies of Einstein. This is my favorite Einstein story.

Shortly before Einstein's death, he realized he had very limited time left. He wrote to many of his former students, colleagues, and friends. He had decided to have a final audience with them in Princeton, New Jersey. He wanted to set up a situation wherein they could ask him any question about his work, his life, and his view of the future. He promised to answer any question, personal or scientific.

Around 300 people responded and, aware that Einstein's energy was limited by his age and condition, they arranged to get together three days before the meeting. Their purpose was to sort out and prioritize their questions so that they would (1) not overtax this generous genius and (2) make sure the more important questions were answered first.

As the story goes, they rented a hotel in Princeton. For the first two and a half days, they did nothing but argue about which questions should be asked first. During the afternoon of the third day, a brilliant scientist from Europe proposed that, with no real prospect for agreement about which questions were the most important, they should ask the "old man himself" to designate the most important question they could ask.

18

That idea broke the stalemate and brought agreement to the group. Most of those attending suspected that Einstein would propose a question about his current interest, the Unified Field Theory.

The next morning, Einstein sat on the stage, in a rocking chair, before this audience representing many of the world's most outstanding minds. The moderator asked for quiet and proposed the most agreed-on question: "Dr. Einstein, the first question we would like to ask you is: 'What is the most important question we could ask today?'"

Without hesitation, Einstein replied, "The most important question you could ever ask is: 'Is the Universe a friendly place?'" This was not the reply the audience anticipated, but it *is* the most important question we can ask.

Earlier in the chapter, what animal did you choose as having the characteristics you find in the market? Is the animal friendly and cordial or is it threatening and dangerous? Let's make that question a bit more specific: Is the *market* a friendly place to you? If it is not, then continue to read this book and learn the Profitunity approach to trading. I summarize the overall goal of this book this way:

The market becomes a friendly and supportive place for you.

Let's start our journey to the top of the trading hill. The opportunity, the timing, and the economy are just right for climbing.

2

Understanding the Markets

If you see in any given situation only what everybody else can see, you can be said to be so much a representative of your culture that you are a victim of it.

S. I. Hayakawa

GOAL: TO UNDERSTAND HOW THE FUTURES MARKET REALLY WORKS AND WHY THE MAJORITY OF TRADERS LOSE MONEY

A number of years ago I attended a meeting in Boulder, Colorado, with the newly arrived Swami Muktananda from India. He proved to be a most interesting fellow. He gave no lectures; he only told stories and wove those stories into an instructional format. Accompanying him was an interpreter, complete with saffron-colored robes, from the University of Colorado. Muktananda maintained that not being fluent in English was a great advantage to becoming a guru in America. He started his lecture with the following story.

There was a student in India who wanted to become enlightened. He left his family in search of an appropriate guru to guide him further on his journey. Stopping at one guru's place of business, he inquired as to this guru's method of becoming enlightened. The guru said, "Becoming enlightened is really quite simple. All you need to do is to go home each night and sit in front of a mirror for 30 minutes asking yourself the same question over and over. That question is: 'Who am I? Who am I? Who am I?'" The prospective student replied, "Hey, it can't be that simple."

"Oh yes, it is just that simple," replied the guru, "but if you would like a second opinion, there are several other gurus on this street."

"Thank you very much," said the student, "I think I will inquire down the way."

The student approached the second guru with the same question. "How do I become enlightened?"

The second guru replied, "Oh, it is quite difficult and takes much time. Actually, one must join with like-minded others in an ashram and do *sava*. *Sava* means 'selfless service,' so you work without pay."

The student was excited; this guru's philosophy was more consistent with his own preconceived view of enlightenment. He had always heard it was difficult. The guru told the student that the only job open at the ashram was cleaning out the cow stalls. If the student was really serious about becoming enlightened, the guru would allow him to shovel all the dung and be responsible for keeping the cow stalls clean. The student accepted the job, feeling confident that he must be on the right path.

After five long years of shoveling cow dung and keeping the stalls clean, the student was becoming discouraged and impatient about enlightenment. He approached the guru and said, "Honored teacher, I have faithfully served you for five years cleaning up the dirtiest part of your ashram. I have never missed a day and have never complained once. Do you think it might be time for me to become enlightened?"

The guru answered, "Why yes, I believe you are ready. Now, here is what you do. You go home every night and look yourself in the mirror for 30 minutes, asking yourself the same question over and over. That question is: 'Who am I? Who am I? Who am I?'"

The very surprised student said, "Pardon me, honored one, but that is what the other guru down the street told me five years ago."

"Well, he was right," responded the guru.

I think of that story quite often while trading. I devote part of my time to training other people to become full-time professional traders. I have privately trained over 450 people who are now trading their own accounts full-time. Over the past ten years, I have spoken to over 20,000 traders in groups and workshops in many different countries. One of the first problems I encounter is in convincing them that making profits in trading is really quite simple—notice, I did not say *easy*. There is a world of difference between a concept's being simple and being easy to carry out.

Looking at yourself in a mirror for 30 minutes each night is a simple concept, but asking yourself the same question over and over and seeking an honest answer is not easy. As a psychologist, I believe that we humans have two innate tendencies: (1) we tend to *overcomplicate* everything we touch and, because of that, (2) we cannot see the obvious. Let's look at what markets *really* are. There is no reason to spend years with no pay (profits) dealing with the cow dung of current losing concepts about the trading market.

To most traders, the market is a dangerous and undependable animal. Their mottoes are: Don't Count on It, and Get It before It Gets You. They see the market as a dog-eat-dog world where other traders are the dogs. That is not an accurate picture of the market.

This chapter examines how simple *all* markets really are. We'll look at some good reasons to be interested in trading as a career, and we'll see why the maps we were taught to use in school don't work in the futures market. Our cultural heritage works against us rather than being an asset.

THE SIMPLICITY OF ALL MARKETS

The primary purpose of commodity markets is to ration, at a reasonable price, existing and future supply to those who want it the most. Trading is not something mysterious and unfathomable. You trade almost every minute of the day.

Trading is really simple (again, I didn't say *easy*). Let's illustrate this with what A. P. Pacelli (1989) calls the Flintstone market. You remember Fred Flintstone, a rather rough and outdoors kind of guy, and his more domestic next-door neighbor, Barney. Fred sees himself as a macho he-man who likes to hunt dinosaurs. One day he goes out and kills a big somethingsaurus. His freezer is already full of dinosaur burgers. Barney does not enjoy hunting and killing but he likes eating dinosaur burgers. Barney prefers to sit around his backyard whittling wood and making clubs.

Fred wanders over to Barney's backyard and gets an idea. Why not swap Barney a couple of platters of dinosaur burgers for that new club he is finishing. Fred rarely takes time to make his own clubs. He'd rather hunt. So he puts this proposition to Barney: "Barney, I'll give you two platters of dinosaur burgers for that new club. How about it?" Barney says, "OK, you got a deal."

Fred and Barney have created a commodity market. *It is just that simple.* All commodity markets in the world are based on one principle that is the basis of all trading:

All commodity markets are created by people who disagree on value and agree on price!!!!

Barney would rather have the dinosaur burgers than the club, and Fred would rather have the club than the two platters of burgers. They agree on price and disagree on value. When you bought your last car, the car was worth more to you than the money you paid for it. However, to the person who sold you the car, your money was more valuable than the car. You created a miniature commodity market when you made your deal.

We buy bonds when we would rather own the bonds than hold onto the money we're paying for them. Our fantasy (trading is a fantasy game; more about this later) is that the "value" of the bonds will go up. We buy them from some unknown trader who is just as sure that their value will go down. We have a real disagreement on current and future value, but we agree on price.

Every market in the world is designed to ration or distribute a limited amount of some commodity (whether agricultural, financial, or whatever) to those who want it most. The market does this by finding and defining the exact price where, at that moment, there is an *absolute balance between the power of those who want to buy and those who want to sell.*

The commodity markets find that place of balance very quickly. They find it before you and I can detect any imbalance and before the traders on the floor become aware of the imbalance. If the above scenario is true, then we must come to some very simple and important conclusions about information that is distributed through the market and accepted without question.

The first thing we can throw out of our tool bag is bullish and bearish consensus. If the markets are doing their job (and they do it well), there can be no such thing as bearish or bullish consensus. Those who tout the bull–bear information get it by surveying a group of traders and asking them their opinion about the market. If, for example, they report a 75 percent bullish consensus in bonds, that means they haven't surveyed all the bears. The markets cannot endure even 50.01 percent bullishness before the price rises.

If there is no such thing as bullish or bearish consensus, then it logically follows that there cannot be any such thing as an oversold or overbought condition, even though analysts talk about it all day on CNBC-FNN and have an oscillator that supposedly measures it. How can it be measured when the market will destroy any oversold or overbought situations in seconds, well before the audience sees it on the TV screen?

Let's examine some other paradoxical misconceptions. Two often repeated formulas for successful trading are: (1) Buy low and sell high, and (2) To make profits, trade with the trend. These two statements are absolutely incompatible. If you buy low or sell high, you are standing in the way of the trend, not following it. And if you follow the trend, you are not buying low or selling high.

I agree with Mark Twain, who supposedly said, "I am less and less interested in what's so and more and more interested in not believing what's not so."

As we start eliminating these misconceptions, we can begin to see the market as it really is. Trading becomes a more profitable occupation when it is based on reality rather than on someone else's imagination.

THE RISKY ROAD TO PERSONAL AND FINANCIAL FREEDOM

Why would anyone be interested in a risky business like trading? Why does it have such attraction? One reason is that trading commodities may be the last bastion of free enterprise. The profit potential is unlimited. If you have owned your own business, you have experienced the downside of motivating workers and dealt with governmental taxes and regulations. You know that the success or failure of your business can be affected by others, in ways that are outside your control.

If you are employed by a small business or a large corporation, you know about difficult managers, salary limitations, and the risk of job loss. Even if you are a professional charging hundreds of dollars an hour, your income is still limited by the number of hours you can work per week.

In contrast, trading futures offers you personal and financial freedom. You can live and work wherever you choose. No one tells you when to be at the office or when you can take a vacation. You report to no one but yourself.

A good trader increases income by adding contracts. The amounts of work and of time are the same, but the payoff for staying at home and placing telephone calls to the trading floor or to a broker can be very rewarding.

Unlike buying and selling stocks on margin (you pay interest), in commodities, you can put most of the money in your account into T-bills or overnight money markets (you receive interest) while using 80 percent of the T-bills and 100 percent of the money markets as trading margin.

In trading your account, there are no consumer problems, no customer relations, no complaints, no theft, no returns, no unions, no employee benefit plans, no stockholders, and no boring board of director's meetings. You won't have to worry about advertising costs, employees, service calls, repairs, or returned or damaged goods.

Why doesn't this list of freedoms attract hordes of people? It does; and 90+ percent of them end up as losers. The other side of the profitability coin is that the winners will always have an ample supply of traders who, because they don't understand the market, will furnish the winners with profits.

Warren Buffett expressed this eloquently, in comparing a poker game with trading: "If you are in a poker game for twenty minutes and you don't know who the patsy is—*you* are the patsy. If you are in a commodity trade for twenty minutes and you don't know who the paymaster is—*you* are the paymaster." One purpose of this book is to make you patsy-proof and keep you from being the paymaster in your trades.

Most people are negative about trading the market. They feel this is a high-risk career because only a small percentage of traders are consistently profitable.

What they don't hear is that traders who do not listen to brokers, do not read newsletters and the *Wall Street Journal,* do not consult CNBC-FNN and similar sources, can be highly successful. Listen to the media or let your broker steer your account, and you'll be back at work in no time.

There *is* risk in trading. There is also enormous risk whenever you drive your car. On some highways, only inches separate your car from the cars speeding in the opposite direction. A swerve of only a few feet could bring a death-dealing head-on collision. Every time you take a short drive, you are literally risking your life. Yet you drive almost daily and remain suave about the danger. The reasons: you have gained *understanding* and *experience.*

As you gain understanding and experience in trading, the markets need be no more dangerous than the route of your Sunday drive. For safe driving, you must have a vehicle you are familiar with, the right tools in case repairs are needed, and the right attitude. That is what this book is all about: having the right understanding and the right attitude for using the right tools.

THE WRONG MAP

Most traders lose because *they* are lost, and they are using the wrong maps. I live in Mobile, Alabama, where Mardi Gras celebration is years older than the more famous New Orleans Mardi Gras. We recently had a friend inquire about visiting us and then going on to the New Orleans Mardi Gras. When he inquired if we had a map of New Orleans, I jokingly said no but that's OK because I do have a map of Mobile. He thought I had lost my marbles until I pointed out the similarities in geography between New Orleans and Mobile. New Orleans has a river running through downtown; so does Mobile. New Orleans has a large lake on the outskirts; so does Mobile. New Orleans is close to the Gulf of Mexico; so is Mobile. Geographically, they are very much alike. I am much more familiar with the Mobile map than the New Orleans map, and I've been using the Mobile map for years.

Had my friend taken my advice and attempted to find Bourbon Street using a Mobile map, he never would have arrived at Bourbon Street. He most likely would have gone the wrong way on one-way streets and found himself at the end of dead-end roads. Similarly, most traders go wrong because they attempt to navigate the market by referring to *wrong maps.*

The right kind of map for the market is not a map of territory but a *cultural logic map.* Your cultural logic affects everything you do—your speech, your thinking, your behavior, how you eat, how you enjoy sex, and how you trade. Your perceptions of all your activities depend on the cultural logic map you are using.

Historically, our current cultural logic map started around 500 B.C., in a gigantic cultural revolution starring Plato, Socrates, Aristotle, Heraclitus, Demosthenes, Euclid, and others. A philosophical war was going on, especially between students of Aristotle and Heraclitus. Aristotle seduced the intellectual world with the idea that if you don't know something, your best bet is to go to someone who knows more than you and ask him or her some questions. That makes sense but, as we will see later, it may not be the best map for trading. Heraclitus's most famous saying translates to: "You can't step into the same river twice. No matter how fast you put your foot into the water, withdraw it and put it in again, not only has the river moved but your foot has also changed."

Because our ancestors selected the Aristotelian approach, we have the precedent system in our law courts, the "scientific method" that acknowledges only experiments that are "repeatable," and the "double-blind" studies in medicine. Aristotelian logic affects our perception of and interaction with the world at every step.

Euclid, around 500 B.C., developed what is now called plane geometry. He never meant it to be a "description of nature." He designed Euclidean geometry to be a report card for art. During his lifetime, art was flourishing and the value of a piece of art depended mainly on personal bias. Euclid came up with laws of proportion and balance, for more consistent standards to evaluate the art of that day. The laws were never designed to be used in surveying or navigation.

One of the "laws" of triangles is that "the interior angles of any triangle will always total 180 degrees, no matter what the shape of the triangle." That is true, but *only* in the gravitational field of the earth. As a spaceship leaves the earth's gravitational field on its way to the moon, the total becomes more than 180 degrees because of the curvature of space. For us, that variation doesn't matter; most of us will not go to the moon. The point, however, is that the law of triangles is a specific truth and not a universal truth. That concept will become extremely important as we do an in-depth study of our market maps.

In the history of humans, there seems to be a cataclysmic change about every 500 years. About five centuries after the renaissance in Greece came the birth of Christianity, and about five centuries later the Roman Empire fell to barbarian invaders.

During the centuries that followed (the so-called Dark Ages), the Catholic Church preserved most of our Western culture's knowledge. The Vatican Library has been the main repository of the manuscripts that were the sources of learning. At that time, the Church believed that only priests should be taught to read because only they had the training to properly interpret the scriptures. Churchmen felt they had received all the Truth straight from God, and were not motivated to explore more of the unknown in search of further and newer truths. Their perceived mission of keeping heathens, heretics, and infidels from polluting "the Truth" produced the Crusades, the Inquisition, and notorious witch hunts. What is more important here, their rigid definition of acceptable knowledge affected the way that people, even today, believe the world to be.

Copernicus and Galileo were hampered in their scientific explorations by a consensus of what was proper to investigate. Around 1500 A.D., the big news was gun powder and movable type. Knowledge began to spread all over the world at a previously impossible speed. Political and Church power began to dwindle as common individuals' knowledge began to increase.

Isaac Newton made the connection between a falling apple and gravity. Even as he drew a slightly more sophisticated picture of natural phenomena, he was still entombed by the culture of his day. Classical physics developed within the confines of the same logic map. The "scientific method" handed down from Aristotle became the accepted method for the search for and the definition of relevant knowledge.

Traditional science, which created automobiles, factories, air and space travel, computers, and many other advances, turns out to be impotent in two vital areas: (1) living systems and (2) turbulence. Classical physics can describe every nanosecond since the "big bang," but it cannot approach any explanation of blood running through the left ventricle of the heart, the turbulence in a white-water river, or the tasseling of corn. If the market is anything, it is living systems (human traders) working in turbulence (the market).

Physics in the 20th century will be remembered for three revolutionary developments: (1) relativity, (2) quantum mechanics, and (3) the science of chaos. Einstein left us with only one constant—the speed of light. Quantum mechanics took that away. Now, the science of chaos is changing our entire worldview.

Look at it this way. The room where you are as you read this page likely has straight lines and flat walls, which you almost never find in nature (with a few exceptions in crystalline deposits).

We have developed a whole set of mathematics under the crippled logic of our evolving, developing brain. This logic leaves immense areas of our world undiscoverable and indescribable. Recently, a new look at the world, a science of chaos, has been emerging. Chaos is a particularly unfortunate name because chaos actually refers to a higher degree of *order*.

We will look more closely at the science of chaos in the next chapter and will then examine the underlying structure of the market and how it yields much better indicators than traditional technical or fundamental analysis does.

SUMMARY

The market is simple. Quickly and efficiently, it finds that point where there is *equal disagreement on value, and agreement on price.* We illustrated that concept with the "Flintstone market" and the trade between Barney and Fred.

Two large problems still face any new trader. First, most traders (90% of all traders) are using the wrong logic maps. Second, there are no consistent, effective, currently available techniques for precisely directing one's energy to move from the level of novice trader to expert trader. In the next chapter, we will examine the new science of chaos, fractal geometry, and their contributions to trading.

3

Chaos Theory: A New Paradigm for Trading

It's well known that the heart has to be largely regular or you die. But the brain has to be largely irregular; if not, you have epilepsy. This shows that irregularity, chaos, leads to complex systems. It's not all disorder. On the contrary, I would say chaos is what makes life and intelligence possible. *The brain has been selected to become so unstable that the smallest effect can lead to the formation of order.*

Ilya Prigogine

GOAL: TO GAIN A BETTER UNDERSTANDING OF CHAOS AND FRACTAL GEOMETRY

The word *paradigm* comes from the Greek root *paradeigma*, which means "model or pattern." Adam Smith, in his book, *Powers of the Mind* (1975), defines a paradigm as "a shared set of assumptions." Smith continues, "The paradigm is the way we perceive the world; it is water to the fish. The paradigm explains the world to us and helps us to predict its behavior" (p. 20).

Social paradigms determine our behavior and values. Medical paradigms determine how we think about our bodies. Our paradigms about the market both determine and limit our interaction with the market.

32

A paradigm is the filter through which we view the world. It is our view of "reality." And because it determines our reality, we rarely notice it and even more rarely question it. Our personal paradigms determine our personal reality and our assumptions about our world. We do not think about these assumptions, we think *from* them.

We never see the world directly; we always see it through these paradigm filters. We never see the world in its entirety; we see only pieces. The same is true with the market. We never see it all; we see only pieces of it. And our mental frameworks naturally bias us toward seeing only those parts of the world (market) that support our paradigms.

Paradigms also filter incoming information, which tends to reinforce comfortable preexisting paradigms (belief systems and mental programs). That's why the market is like the Grand Canyon. If you shout into it, "*Technical analysis!*," the echo you get back is "Technical analysis." If you shout, "*Astrology!*," you hear "Astrology." If you shout "*Chaos!*," you hear "Chaos."

This calls into question the notion of a fixed objective universe (market). Just as an object appears differently in infrared light, in ordinary daylight, or on an X-ray negative, how reality (the market) appears to us has less to do with what is actually there than with how we perceive it.

Adam Smith pointed out: "When we are in the middle of a paradigm it is hard to imagine any other paradigm" (p. 20). For example, suppose it is 1968 and you are asked to predict the world leader in watch manufacturing in the 1980s. You say the Swiss, because they have dominated the watch market for so many years. However, a paradigm shift occurs, from mechanical watches to electronic watches. The Japanese, because they recognize the new paradigm, capture most of the world's watch market. The Swiss, by clinging to the old paradigm, steadily lose their market share of more than 90 percent in 1968 and hit a low of below 10 percent during the 1980s. Ironically, the Swiss invented the quartz watch in the first place. Whenever there is a paradigm shift, all the rules change. In a wrong paradigm, even the right actions don't work.

Our personal paradigms control the way we process and respond to information. Your feelings or paradigms of viewing the markets are very different after you pick ten consecutive losers as opposed to ten consecutive winners. The following story illustrates how drastically and quickly our paradigms may change.

There is a Hollywood actor who likes to get away to his cabin in the mountains each weekend. He drives there over curvy, mountainous dirt roads. He usually drives his Porsche convertible and enjoys seeing how fast he can take the curves. He rarely meets anyone on these roads because there are few cabins in the area and even fewer visitors.

One Friday afternoon as he zooms through these curves, he meets an oncoming car that has careened over into his lane. There is a substantial cliff to his right, so he brakes his Porsche as hard as he can and stops just before a head-on collision.

The other car is also a convertible. The driver pulls around his stopped Porsche, she guns her engine, points, and shouts "PIG." This puzzles him. He was in his lane, it certainly wasn't his fault, and he was not "hogging" the road. As she drives off in a cloud of dust, he turns and shouts loudly, "SOW!"

Now he is fuming. He floors the accelerator, gains speed around the next curve, and collides with a large hog standing in the middle of the road. His interpretation of the other driver's motives and behavior changes immediately. His response had come not from what she said but from his personal paradigm.

The particular paradigm through which we view the market determines our feelings and our behavior. The science of chaos gives us a new and more appropriate paradigm (map) to view the world, the markets, and our personal behavior.

Let's look at this new paradigm, try to understand it better, and begin to make the connection of how we can use it to get a more accurate picture of market behavior.

CHAOS AND OUR PERSONAL WORLD

We humans have a habit of misnaming our most important concerns and tools. For example, what we call our "conscious" mind (left hemisphere) is the only part of our brain that ever goes "un-conscious" or sleeps. The other parts of our brain work continuously without a break. Similarly, physicists have chosen to call this new science chaos, a term that is fundamentally misleading.

Chaos does not refer to randomness; just the opposite is true. Chaos is a higher form of order where randomness and stimuli become the organizing principle rather than the more traditional "cause and effect" in the Newtonian/Euclidean sense. Because both nature and the human brain are chaotic, the markets, as a part of nature and a reflection of human nature, are chaotic as well. It is time to recognize that our standard education gives traders the wrong impression and the wrong logic maps. No matter how elaborate linear mathematics gets, with its Fourier transforms, orthogonal functions, regression techniques, artificial intelligence, neural networks, genetic algorithms, and so on, it inevitably misleads traders about their overwhelmingly nonlinear markets. The markets are connoisseurs of chaos.

The
normal
distribution
stands out in the
experience of humankind
as one of the broadest generalizations
of natural science. It has been used as a
trading instrument in the markets, in the physical
and social sciences, and in medicine, agriculture, and
engineering. It is an indispensable tool for the analysis and
the interpretation of the basic data gathered by observation.

35

The structure of the previous three sentences represents the Gaussian or normal distribution curve. It makes a statement about the nature of randomness. But as a means of finding one's way through the wilderness of trading, this standard leaves much to be desired. As Nobel laureate Wassily Leontief put it, "In no field of empirical inquiry has so massive and sophisticated a statistical machinery been used with such indifferent results" (quoted in Gleick, 1987, p. 84).

Commodity prices simply do not fit the bell-shaped model. They do, however, make some configurations that look amazingly like figures in other places such as shorelines and riverbeds. Benoît Mandelbrot, at the IBM research center at Yorktown Heights, New York, worked with masses of cotton price data. He was looking for some common parameters between nature and human behavior. He found that numbers producing aberrations from the point of view of normal distribution produced symmetry from the point of view of scaling. "Each particular price change was random and unpredictable. But the sequence of changes was independent of scale: curves for the daily and monthly price changes matched perfectly. Incredibly, analyzed Mandelbrot's way, the degree of variation had remained constant over a tumultuous sixty-year period that saw two World Wars and a depression" (Gleick, 1987, p. 86).

Chaos is not new, it has been around since before time and humankind. We are the products of chaos, not the inventors of it. Chaos is what got us here and chaos will take us further into the future. Even in our brain, one part (left hemisphere) is looking for stability and another part (right hemisphere) is looking for chaos. We (self, body, personality, and all) have developed on that tricky interface between stability and chaos.

Chaos is the meeting ground between yin/yang, black/white, here/there, now/then, or our development. In shaman terms, it is the tonal and the nagel. In markets, it is choppy versus trending. In trader's behavior, it is winning and losing. It is sleeping and waking, planting and harvesting.

Figure 3–1 shows the transformation from linear flow to nonlinear or turbulent flow. In Figure 3–1(a), the stream is moving in a very stable fashion and is quite predictable. Figure 3–1(b) shows more water running; turbulence is beginning to build up behind the rock. Add more water (energy in the form

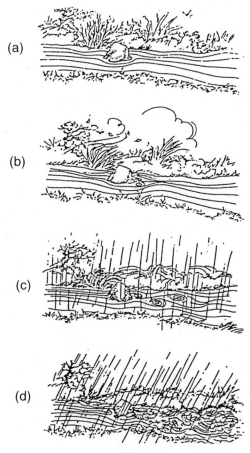

Figure 3–1   From order to chaos.

of rain and gravity), and the turbulence increases and there is less predictability in the stream (Figure 3–1(c) and (d)).

Our brain also develops different behavior, depending on the flow of energy. It is sometimes stable, like the stream in Figure 3-1(a). When trading the market, it is often turbulent, like the stream in Figure 3–1(d).

Since Aristotle's time, we have spent much more time educating and using the stable (left hemisphere linear) part rather than the chaos (right hemisphere nonlinear) part of our brain. According to our current linear logic map, "truth" lies in stability or never-changing knowledge, so there is little benefit in developing a strategy for dealing with or using chaos.

Nonlinear logic makes it obvious that stability is temporary and chaos is forever. Over the past 10 years, millions of dollars have been "thrown" at the concept of chaos in attempts to, first, make sense of the markets, and second, profit from that knowledge. Research has made an effort to better understand chaos and the interaction between the mass of traders and the market itself. Our research finds that the Chaos of our minds is reflected in the market. Both are an elaborate mixture of Chaos and stability. Prigogine has written: "The brain is a creature of chaos, a far from equilibrium soup simmering on an uneven flame of daily life" (Prigogine and Stengers, I., 1984, p. 48).

Stability and chaos are also described as linear and nonlinear activity, whether that activity involves growing, producing, reproducing, or even just thinking. If we were to create the world from our left hemisphere perspective, we would have straight rivers, round clouds, and cone-shaped mountains. Nature, however, had other forces. Our natural world came from nonlinear sources. Man-made products such as language came from the left hemisphere and consequently are digital and linear. We have created our trading systems in the same way we created language, and just as language is not successful in describing nature, so linear trading systems are unsuccessful in describing and capturing profits from the market. Remember, chaos got us here and chaos will take us where we want to go.

FRACTAL GEOMETRY

The science of chaos represents considerably more than a new trading technique. It is a new way of viewing our world. This worldview is actually older than recorded history but, until the mid-1970s, we lacked the powerful computers or other equipment needed to deal with this worldview on a mathematical and functional basis. Chaos theory is the first approach that successfully models complex forms (living and nonliving) and turbulent flows with rigorous mathematical methodology.

Fractal geometry, one of the tools of the science of chaos, is used to study phenomena that are chaotic only from the perspective of Euclidean geometry and linear mathematics.

Fractal analysis has revolutionized research in a myriad of different fields such as meteorology, geology, medicine, markets, and metaphysics. This startlingly new perspective will profoundly affect all of us for the rest of our lives. Fractal analysis is a powerful new paradigm that, together with quantum mechanics and relativity theory, completes the scientific world first glimpsed by Galileo.

Although classical physics can model the creation of the universe from the first one-thousandth of a second of the "big bang" to the present time, it cannot model the blood flow through the left ventricle of a human heart for one second. Classical physics can model the structure of matter from subatomic quarks to galaxy clusters, but cannot model the shape of a cloud, the structure of a plant, the flow of a river, or the machinations of the market.

Science is very comfortable with its ability to create models using linear mathematics and Euclidean geometry. It is not, however, impressive in dealing with nonlinear turbulence and living systems. Simply stated, a nonlinear effect occurs when the power of an effect is a multiple of the power of the cause. There is an absolute chain between cause and effect in the Newtonian world, and all shapes are smooth and regular in Euclidean geometry. Neither of these approaches can begin to explain market behavior.

The smooth and frictionless surfaces, the empty space, the perfect spheres, cones, and right angles of Euclidean geometry are aesthetically appealing, even soothing. They are not, however, descriptive of the rough, jagged world in which we live and trade.

From this Euclidean/Newtonian world, we developed our linear mathematics, including parametric statistics most often symbolized by the "normal" or bell-shaped curve. This approach facilitates understanding by simplifying and abstracting out elements we think are unessential to the system. The key word here is *unessential*. In the real world, these discarded "unessentials" do not represent unimportant deviation from the Euclidean norm; rather, they represent the essential character of these systems. By abstracting out these unessential deviations (now known as fractals) from the norm, we are able to glimpse the real underlying structure of energy and behavior.

As Benoit Mandelbrot, who first coined the term fractal, so aptly put it:

> Why is geometry often described as cold and dry? One reason lies in its inability to describe the shape of a cloud, a mountain, a coastline, a tree. Clouds are not spheres, mountains are not cones, coastlines are not circles, and bark is not smooth, nor does the lightning travel in a straight line. . . . Nature exhibits not simply a higher degree but an altogether different level of complexity. The number of distinct scales of length of patterns is for all purposes infinite. The existence of these patterns challenges us to study these forms that Euclid leaves aside as being formless, to investigate the morphology of the morphous.

Mathematicians have disdained this challenge, however, and have increasingly chosen to flee from nature by devising theories unrelated to anything we can see or feel. (quoted in Gleick, 1987, p. 98)

Mandelbrot and other scientists such as Prigogine, Feigenbaum, Barnsley, Smale, and Henon found incredible revelations in this new approach to studying both inanimate and living behavior. They discovered that at the boundary line between conflicting forces is not the birth of chaos, as previously thought, but the spontaneous emergence of self-organization on a higher scale. Moreover, this self-organization is not structured along the Euclidean/Newtonian pathways but is a new kind of organization. It is not static but rather is imbedded in the fabric of motion and growth. It seems to be relevant to everything from lightning bolts to markets.

This new internal structure is found in the exact spots that earlier researchers had labeled random (nonessential) and discarded. The stages marking the onset of turbulence—and their timing and intensity—can now be predicted with more exact mathematical precision.

The themes that emerge are: order exists within chaos, and chaos gives birth to order. To get a better fundamental grasp of this change in perspective, let's look at a typical problem with linear analysis. We can then begin to apply this new approach to trading.

How Can We Measure the Length of a Coastline?

Lewis F. Richardson, an English scientist, first addressed the problem of calculating the length of a coastline or of any national border. The problem was solved later by Mandelbrot. At first glance, this seems a silly problem, but it actually raises very serious issues concerning the viability of Euclidean measurement for certain classes of objects and for the markets.

41

Imagine that you are assigned the task of measuring the coastline of Florida. Your boss wants an accurate measurement and gives you a ten-foot-long rod. You walk the perimeter of the peninsula. You finish your work and calculate your answer. Then your boss decides that the ten-foot rod missed too much detail. You are given a yardstick and instructed to repeat the process. You redo your work and come up with a much larger measurement. Using a one-foot ruler would yield an even longer measurement for the coastline, and if you could use a one-inch ruler and still keep your sanity, your answer would rise toward infinity. The shorter the measuring device, the more detail is captured. A coastline is representative of a class of objects having an infinite length in a finite space.

The length of a coastline is not a measurable quantity in the Euclidean approach to measurement. If Florida had a smooth Euclidean shape, there would be a fixed answer to the question of its length. But virtually all natural shapes are irregular. They defy absolute values of traditional measurement.

Mandelbrot invented a new way of measuring such irregular natural objects or natural systems. He named it the fractal or, more properly, the fractional dimension. The fractional dimension is the degree of roughness or irregularity of a structure or system. Mandelbrot found that the fractional dimension remains constant over different degrees of magnification of an irregular object. In other words, there is regularity in all irregularity. When we normally refer to an occurrence as random, we indicate that we don't understand the structure of that randomness. In market terms, this means that the same pattern formation should exist in different time frames. A one-minute chart will contain the same fractal pattern as a monthly chart. This "self-similarity" found in commodity and stock charts gives further indication that market action is more closely attuned to the paradigm of "natural" behavior rather than economic, fundamental, mechanical, or technical behavior.

Mandelbrot also found a close similarity between the fractal number of the Mississippi River and cotton prices over all the time periods he studied, which included world wars, floods, droughts, and similar disasters. The profoundness of this observation cannot be overstated. It means that the markets are a "natural" nonlinear function and not a "classical physics" linear function, and it explains, at least partially, why 90 percent of traders using technical analysis lose consistently. Not only is technical analysis based on the false assumption that the future will be like the past, but it uses inappropriate linear techniques for analysis.

Just as Euclidean analysis cannot accurately measure the coastline of Florida, neither can it accurately measure the behavior of a market. In our analysis of Level Two trading (in Chapter 7), we will examine precisely how to trade this behavior. In Chapter 12, we will examine our own internal fractal structure; indeed, the human body may very well be the richest source of fractal structures in existence. The electrical activity of the heart is a fractal process. So is the immune system. The bronchial tubes, lungs, liver, kidneys, and circulatory system are all fractal structures. The entire physical structure of humans seems to be fractal in nature; perhaps most importantly, the human brain is fractal in structure. It is theorized that, to work at all, humans' memory, thinking process, and self-awareness must all be fractal in structure and functioning.

Given the above, it would be reasonable to theorize that any pattern that was the result of human interaction (e.g., the markets) should also be fractal in structure. The market is a product of mass psychology and the composite of individual traders' fractal structure. This means that the market is generated by turbulent collective activity and is a nonlinear phenomenon.

Any trader with a bit of experience has learned that the markets are not a simple, mechanical result of supply and demand. If humans were machines, price action would be a simple two-basin attractor system of supply and demand forces. A pendulum hung between two magnets is a simple two-basin attractor system (see Figure 3–2). Two-basin attractors are simple, linear, and boring. A two-basin market would have no complexity, nonlinearity, turbulence, or volatility.

If a third attractor is placed near the pendulum, chaos or fractal structure is introduced to the system. In our own modeling, we have delineated five different magnetic attractors that affect the price movement from one basin to another. The system is nonlinear, dynamic, and chaotic. And it works.

Because the markets are a nonlinear, turbulent system produced by the interaction of human beings, price and time actions are the perfect places to seek fractal structures. Time and again, turbulent processes in nature produce magnificent structures of complexity, without randomness, in which self-similarity can be observed. Finding the fractal structure of the market produces a way to understand the behavior of the system—that is, the price movement of a particular commodity. It is a way to see pattern, order, and, most important, predictability where others see only chaos.

The primary purpose of this book is to show you how to trade using fractal geometry. Twelve years of intensive research have been dedicated to the fractal geometry of the markets.

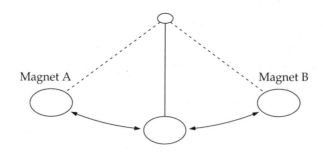

Figure 3–2   A two-basin attractor.

Without boring you with details of this research, let's look at just one example of how fractal analysis contributes to better understanding of the trading tools for the market.

Fractals are produced on computer screens by using a process called iteration. Accretion is a nonsystematic iteration. Something is added to something else, and that bigger thing is added to something else, and so on. The simplest model of iteration is the summation sequence known as the Fibonacci numbers. The sequence starts with 0, and the first two terms added are 1 and 1. Add 1 to the starting 0, and the answer is 1. Add the second 1, and the answer is 2. From that point, the two immediately preceding numbers are added together to get the next number in the sequence. So, add 1 and 2, and the answer is 3. Add 2 and 3, and the answer is 5. Add 3 and 5, and the answer is 8. Add 5 and 8, and the answer is 13. The sequence continues to infinity. The curious property of this iteration process is that each number in the sequence is exactly .618 of the next number, no matter what two numbers in the sequence one examines. The .618 ratio is the invariant product of systematic accretion.

The world is awash with .618 relationships. Seed patterns on flowers are Fibonacci numbers. The heart muscle contracts to exactly .618 of its resting length. The perfect .618 structure is exemplified by the Nautilus shell. A more personal example is the human navel, located at .618 of a person's height. Volumes have been written simply listing and categorizing incidences in nature of this .618 phenomenon.

The Rosetta Stone of fractal geometry is the Mandelbrot set, shown in Figure 3–3. The Mandelbrot set, the master fractal and the building block of fractal geometry, is produced by graphing the numbers resulting from the iteration of a second-degree polynomial on the complex plane.

The Mandelbrot set is structured in Fibonacci .618 relationships. It is composed almost exclusively of spirals and helixes. If you take a nautilus shell, stand it on end, and butterfly it as

45

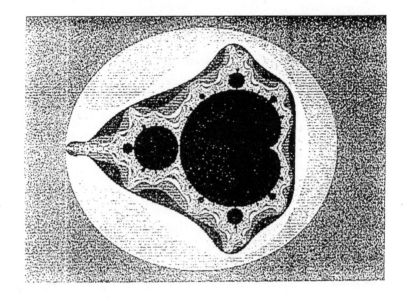

Figure 3–3   Mandelbrot set.

you would a steak, you will get a figure very similar to the Mandelbrot set. This may very well be the keystone that connects Fibonacci numbers, the Elliott wave, and fractals into one coherent paradigm.

In our own original research, the Profitunity Trading Group has discovered several repeating patterns that allow a degree of predictability about future market movements that are quantum leaps ahead of the accepted current technical analysis. These will be discussed in later chapters.

Fractal Geometry and the Markets

Wherever chaos, turbulence, living systems, and disorder are found, fractal geometry is at work. As noted above, fractal actually means a fractional dimension. Imagine you are looking at a three-inch ball of twine from 200 yards away. It will look like a dot, and a dot has zero dimension. Now imagine you are walking up toward the ball of twine. You notice that it is, indeed, a ball of twine and thus has three dimensions. As you approach more closely, you see it is in reality made up of one long string that has only one dimension. By using a magnifying glass and looking even closer, you see that the string itself is actually three dimensional. So, depending on your perspective, you have seen zero dimension, then three dimensions, then one, and then back to three. What you see in the market depends just as much on your perspective or your current paradigm. Actually, your current perspective *is* your paradigm. If you are coming from a linear perspective, you will never see the "real" market and will be at a disadvantage when it comes to trading and making profits.

The fractal is also a measure of irregularity. The more irregular and choppy a market is, the larger will be its fractal number. The fractal number of a portion of a move will always peak at the turnaround point. Therefore, all market trend changes are accompanied by a higher fractal number than the bars leading up to the change in trend.

Figure 3–4 shows British scientist Michael Batty's generation of a fractal tree via a computer. Each branch splits into two

Figure 3–4   Computer-generated fractal tree.

to create a fractal canopy. The illustration on the left has six iterations or bifurcations. By the thirteenth iteration (the illustration on the right), the tree begins to look more realistic. Fractal modelers can produce different species of trees by changing the fractal number. Fractal trees illustrate the point that fractal geometry is a measure of change. Each branching of a tree, each bend in a river, each change of direction in a market is a decision point. This notion became a crucial factor in discovering the "fractal" of the Elliott wave.

CONCLUSION

The science of chaos supplies us with a new and provocative paradigm to view the markets. It provides a more accurate and predictable way to analyze the current and future action of a commodity. It gives us a better map with which to trade. It does not depend on constructing a template from the past and applying it to the future. It concentrates on the current market behavior, which is simply a composite of (and is quite similar to) the individual fractal behavior of the mass of traders. For a more in-depth look at the science of chaos from an academic and research point of view, I suggest the following readings, listed in the Bibliography: Peters (1991a, 1993), Deboeck (1994), and Chorafas (1994). Most of the current research techniques are found in physics and mathematics journals.

The fractal is the underlying structure of both the market and individual traders. In the next chapter, we will examine the two basic types of underlying structures and how they add to our market paradigm.

——— 4 ———

Defining Your Underlying Structure—and How That Affects Winning and Losing

I change not by trying to be
   something other than I am:
I change by becoming
   fully aware of who I am.
Zen theory of existential change

GOAL: TO COMPREHEND THE MARKETS' ENERGY, THE STRUCTURE OF *STRUCTURE*, AND THE TWO TYPES OF UNDERLYING STRUCTURE

As pointed out earlier, one of the primary contributions of the new science of chaos is that it examines "natural phenomena." One of Mandelbrot's pregnant findings was that the fractal dimensions of rivers are similar to those of commodity markets—an indication that the markets are more a function of nature than a process designed by the left hemisphere of the human brain. Our view is that economics, fundamentals, and mechanical and technical analysis do not draw an accurate map of the market's behavior. If the markets were linear, there would be fewer losers—particularly in view of the high intelligence of the average trader. If traditional logic worked, there would be less complaining and more narratives of success.

The science of chaos provides three primary principles for study of the markets. Collectively, these principles govern the behavior of energy. From a physics standpoint, everything in the universe is energy. These principles are discussed fully in Robert Fritz's book, *The Path of Least Resistance* (1989). Let's try to capture their key meanings here.

PRINCIPLES FOR STUDY OF THE MARKETS' ENERGY

1. **Energy always follows the path of least resistance.** A commodity market is like a river. As it moves through each trading minute, it takes the path of least resistance. That's what we all do—not only the market, but you, me, and everything in nature. It is part of the inherent design of nature. While a river is running downstream, its behavior is determined by the path of least resistance. Gravity is energizing it as it flows around rocks and along curves in the riverbed. You are reading this sentence at this time because this was the path of least resistance when all your time management factors were examined. You are sitting wherever you are because that location was on your path of least resistance. In a market, you will exit from a losing trade when the pain of losing one more dollar becomes stronger than the pain of saying that you were wrong in taking the trade. The path of least resistance wins again.

2. **The path of least resistance is determined by the *always underlying* and *usually unseen* structure.** The behavior of a river, whether it is calmly flowing downhill or creating rapids, depends on the underlying structure of the riverbed. If the riverbed is deep and wide, the river will flow calmly down hill.

If the riverbed is shallow and narrow, the riverbed will create rapids. The behavior of the river can be accurately predicted by examining the underlying riverbed.

Suppose you needed to get up and go to the bathroom now. You would most likely walk through one or more rooms or doorways. Why wouldn't you just take a "straight-line" course through the walls to the bathroom? Because you learned long ago that you injure yourself when you walk into walls. As you walk toward the bathroom, you most likely are *unaware* of how your behavior has been determined by the architect who designed the locations of the openings and by the builder who mounted the doors in their present position. The architect and builder gave your rooms their underlying structure.

In the same way, the underlying structure of your life determines your approach to trading. Whether you are aware of the structure or not, it determines your behavior and your reaction to any movement in the market. We will examine this structure in detail in Chapter 9.

Many traders who keep repeating their trading behavior produce losses. They often feel powerless and frustrated. They attend seminars, read books and underline appropriate passages, study NLP (Neuro Linguistic Programming), have private sessions with market psychologists, and then find themselves back in the same old losing rut. If that has happened to you, you simply haven't changed your underlying structure.

If you make only superficial changes, nothing has really changed. Permanent change happens only when the underlying structure is changed. Chapters 6 through 10 examine the underlying structure of the market and advise on how to recognize any change in that underlying structure. Chapters 11 and 12 will help you probe your personal underlying structure. When your personal underlying structure is aligned with that of the market, winning becomes the path of least resistance.

As a trader, you always know when you are trying to go against the path of least resistance. Tension immediately builds up in your body and mind. If you are tense about trading, you are not "floating down the river." Once you learn to determine the underlying structure of a market, you can make peace with the behavior of the market and simply "float like a butterfly, sting like a bee."

3. **This always underlying and usually unseen structure can be discovered and can be altered.** Most traders seem to be trying to change the course of the market/river by using bailing buckets. That task is impossible. However, if they were to hike up the river to its source, they might be able to change the entire course of the river by simply moving a few rocks so that the water flows in a different direction. Sometimes a slight change in cause can produce mammoth changes in behavior. This possibility is not addressed by linear Newtonian/Euclidean physics.

You can change the flow of your life and your trading. To do this easily and permanently, you must work with the underlying structure rather than the behavior produced by that underlying structure.

Once a new and different structure is in place in your trading, the overall thrust of your trading, like the current of a river, builds momentum and aids you in getting the results you want.

The basic concept derived from these three principles is this: you can learn to first recognize the underlying structure that is driving your trading and then change it so that you can create what you really want from the market.

To be able to recognize the underlying structure, we need to examine more closely the structure of *structure*, the keystone to all our results in trading and in life. Later in the chapter, we'll encounter the two types of underlying structure that determine your future behavior and the personality of the path to your goals.

WHAT IS STRUCTURE?

Any structure has four elements: (1) parts (components), (2) plan, (3) power source, and (4) purpose. All structures contain movement and an inclination toward movement; this means they have a tendency to change from one state to another state. Some structures have more tendency toward movement than others do. A more stationary structure is one in which the parts tend to hold each other in check. In a less stationary structure, the parts have a tendency to permit easier movement. A wheelchair has a greater tendency toward movement than a rocking chair does, and a rocking chair has a greater tendency toward movement than a couch does. A couch has a greater tendency toward movement than a building does. In each case, the underlying structure determines the tendency toward movement.

This underlying, usually unseen structure is everywhere in our life and is especially potent in our ever-changing reaction to a changing market.

Edmondson (1992) described the concepts of R. Buckminster Fuller's Synergectic Geometry:

> Thinking isolates events: "understanding" then interconnects them. "Understanding is structure," Fuller declares, for it means establishing the relationship between events.

Structure determines behavior. Structure determines the way anything behaves—a bullet, a hurricane, a cab driver, a spouse, a market. The way the pits are structured determines the behavior of the traders in the pits.

The structures that have the most influence on your trading results are composed of desires, beliefs, assumptions, aspirations, and, most of all, your understanding of the underlying structure of the market and yourself.

This study of structure is independent of and quite different from the study of psychology. However, here is a potent relationship. As you apply structural understanding and principles to your trading, two insights emerge.

First, most of us, probably more because of ignorance than arrogance, have a tendency to ignore nature and simply use it as a backdrop for our more important activities. Traders act according to the underlying structures that rule their entire lives. Since both the markets and the traders are part of nature, it should not be surprising that both act according to "natural" underlying structure. Chaos and fractals are new concepts for most traders. Most see their lives as a struggle against nature or the market rather than as being intimately connected with nature and the market. As the composer Hector Berlioz commented, "Time is the great teacher, but unfortunately it kills all of its students."

The second insight from the study of structures is that some structures produce more and different types of results than others. Structure is impersonal. Some structures lead to pain, no matter who is within the structures. Most traders attempt to change their behavior rather than the structure of their life. They believe that changing their behavior will change the structure. Just the opposite is true. As Robert Fritz notes, "You can't fool Mother Structure."

Some structures lead to final destinations; other structures simply oscillate. Let's examine both types here. Later, we will note the difference each makes when used in the market.

Type One Structure

A Type One structure produces an action–reaction, back-and-forth, figure-eight type of behavior: one type of desired behavior leads into an opposite undesired behavior. A simple example is the pendulum. At the top of its arc, gravity changes its behavior to a downward direction. As it progresses, it builds up momentum. The momentum pushes it downward, past dead center, and toward the opposite side of its arc. Then gravity begins to slow it down. The pendulum loses all the built-up momentum, reaches the top, and begins movement in the opposite direction (Figure 4–1).

Most traders are captured by and operating in Type One structures. For example, suppose you put on a trade and decide to be very conservative with a tight stop. You tell yourself you need the tight stop so that if you are wrong it won't hurt too much. The market has a normal retracement which stops you out; then the market zooms in the direction you thought it would. You analyze your loss and decide that your stops are too close. You must give the market "room to move."

On the next trade, you place your stop unusually far away from your entry, to give the market plenty of "room." The market retreats and gives you a very large loss. You simply cannot withstand this big a loss. Again, in your analysis, you decide to "tighten up your stops."

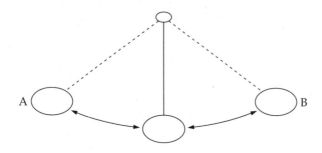

Figure 4–1 Pendulum as type one structure.

The vast majority of losing traders are trapped into this back-and-forth strategy of trading their last mistake. In a Type One structure, change is experienced from time to time but it doesn't last. Any progress turns out to be temporary. A Type One underlying structure makes us vacillate back and forth just like a pendulum. Any time you seem to be getting the same results over and over, you are enmeshed in this Type One structure. Someone once defined insanity as "doing the same thing over and over and expecting different results." If you find yourself on a yo-yo diet, or have quit smoking and still crave cigarettes, or have quit drinking and still want a drink, or want to win and you keep losing, you are in a Type One underlying structure.

If you seek the typical psychotherapist (remember, I have been one) at this point, you will hear words like "self-sabotage," "failure complex," "afraid of succeeding," and so on. The assumption is that inner states of being—emotions, inhibitions, fears—generate your dysfunctional behavior. All of these typical approaches insist that something is wrong with you. The underlying structure here is also Aristotelian and Newtonian: one looks for a "cause," finds a "solution," and brings about a different "effect."

If your underlying structure is one of oscillation, no solution will help because psychological solutions do not address the underlying structure that causes behavior. At times, some of these approaches appear to work, but their effects are temporary. Check out for yourself traders who have used this type of approach; evaluate what percentage of their change has been permanent. Our research clearly shows that the vast majority of traders fall back into their old losing habits. The only permanent change we have found is in those who have altered their underlying structure.

If you are in a pattern of oscillation (remember, all oscillators move around and always come back to zero), do not consider it a problem that you have to overcome. This structure is not adequate to get you to be a consistently winning trader. Fortunately, there is an alternative to this oscillating underlying structure.

Type Two Structure

Notice the natural order of things. Work with it rather than against it for to try to change what is so will only set up resistance.

Zen Proverb

We have identified Type One structure as being based in the left hemisphere of the brain. Type Two structure is located in the creative part of the brain. Type One structure attempts to solve problems (quit losing); Type Two structure is geared for action that brings something new into being. Rather than solving problems, it creates results. The contrast is not unlike the difference between classical physics and quantum physics. Classical physics believes that you have to have something to make something else. Quantum physics maintains that something can be created from nothing. Classical physics say that "stuff" comes from "other stuff." Quantum physics says "stuff" comes from "nonstuff." In Chapter 11, we will put this approach to practical application in realigning our own structure.

When you are successful in solving a problem, all you have is the absence of a problem. You still may not have the result you desire (to be consistently profitable). Our Aristotelian problem-solving mentality has become a way of life. Most of us never consider an alternative approach.

On the national political scene, discussion centers on the problem of the deficit, the problem of inflation, the problem of the homeless, the problem of taxes, the problem of AIDS, the problem of education—ad infinitum. The greatest leaders in history were not problem solvers, they were builders and creators. Franklin Roosevelt and Winston Churchill were not trying to solve the problem of the Axis in World War II; they were building a foundation for the future they wanted for the entire world.

Problem solving certainly has its place, but it has not proven effective in creating winning trading attitudes. Most often, it changes nothing. Here is the key. The path of least resistance in problem solving leads to moving from worse to better and then to worse again. You take action to lessen the intensity of the problem. As the intensity lessens, you exert less effort and less motivation to take further action. This sets up the typical figure-eight pattern where there may be much action but no real progress.

To state this another way, in a problem-solving mode, as soon as you become successful you tend to quit doing the very thing that made you successful in the first place. This sequence is taking place in most businesses today. A new restaurant opens up and offers excellent food to attract patrons, and then falls back to more ordinary cuisine and loses customers. In a romantic relationship, we court each other, put on our best face, are constantly considerate, and make a commitment to marriage. As soon as we are married, we tend to quit doing all those nice little things that made the relationship attractive in the first place. For traders who are trading to solve problems rather than to create profits, the pattern is similar.

Medicine is interested in solving problems rather than creating an extraordinarily healthful existence. Medical science is not a method for creating health. Law is interested in solving the problem of crime rather than rehabilitating those who perform criminal acts. Law is not a method for creating sane civilizations. Psychotherapy, likewise, is not a method of creating peak experiences and personal effectiveness.

Carl Jung (1975), after spending years of dedicated work in this area, concluded that most often the problems themselves were irrelevant. He made this astute observation:

All the greatest and most important problems of life are fundamentally insoluble. . . . They can never be solved, but only out-
grown. This "outgrowth" proved on further investigation to
require a new level of consciousness. Some higher or wider interest appeared on the patient's horizon, and through this broad-
ening of his or her outlook the insoluble problem lost its
urgency. It was not solved logically in its own terms but faded
when confronted with a new and stronger life urge. (p. 29)

Problem solving does not enable you to create what you
want (profits); often, it perpetuates exactly what you don't
want (losses). You don't need to transform your trading—you
need to transcend it.

Type Two structure is a whole other world where everything is *automagically* working for your progress in attaining
your goals. There is little wasted motion or backtracking.
You're at the control of a rocket ship where all the energy is
channeled in the most appropriate direction, and everything
you do seems to contribute to your progress with very little
digression.

Rather than simply problem solving, with Type Two underlying structure you are now on the road to creating. Creating is
a technique you did not learn in school, at home, or on the job.
It is probably the most important skill you can master in order
to trade well. It is very different from reacting or responding to
circumstances. One happy note is that your present circumstances do not in any way limit your creativity in creating profits in trading. The creative process has a different structure
from your reactions or responses to present circumstances.

A trader responding to present circumstances is impris-
oned by them. Circumstances are the walls of your cell. When
you are creating, you are free and your freedom is not threatening to you. All your life you have been told what, when, and
how to do things. Be at work by 9:00, take only an hour for
lunch, and don't leave before 5:00. PTA meeting is Wednesday

night. Doc says I should get eight hours of sleep. I must accomplish the following projects before I'll be considered for that promotion. Quarterly taxes must be in by Friday. Rules and demands come from everywhere.

Now you enter trading, where there are basically *no rules.* You trade when you want, how much you want. You determine your risk. You *create* your profits. The average person has no education or experience to produce this type of results. Traders subscribe to newsletters and hotlines, or camp out with CNBC-FNN in search of guidance. The real guidance can only come from inside, and the results will always be in line with your underlying structure.

We will examine personal underlying structure in detail when we study Level Four in Chapter 11. We will explore the differences between a Type One and a Type Two underlying structure as they affect the markets, you, and your trading. At Level Five, in Chapter 12, we will put the entire package together.

SUMMARY

In this chapter, we have looked at how the world works, both inside and outside your body. We have examined the three principles that are in tune with nature and natural functioning:

1. Everything follows the path of least resistance.

2. This path of least resistance is determined by the always underlying and usually unseen structure.

3. This underlying structure can be discovered and it can be changed.

We then looked deeper into the structure of *structure* and distinguished between the almost universal approach to problem solving versus the more effective and profitable creating type of structure.

In the next chapter, we will examine how humans progress through any learned behavior. We will look at the five steps we all take from being a novice to becoming a master. In subsequent chapters, we will start to take those steps ourselves.

— 5 —

Navigating the Markets: The Need for Good Maps

GOAL: TO STUDY THE UNIVERSAL STEPS FROM NOVICE TO EXPERT AND APPLY THEM TO BECOMING A SUCCESSFUL TRADER

So far, we have discussed the present condition of the majority of traders, looked at how really simple the market is, examined chaos as a more effective trading paradigm, and delved into the two different structures of *structure*. In this chapter, we construct an interactive map that will guide us through the rest of this book. We want explicit directions and feedback that will tell us where we have been, where we are now as traders, and what has to happen for us to improve our trading ability.

THE STAIRWAY TO PROFITS

One of the problems of learning to trade is that there is no regular progression that takes a beginning trader from ignorance to knowledge or from losing to consistent winning. The programs currently available either teach the vocabulary of trading or simply provide a series of favorite indicators. Neither of these approaches produces good consistent traders.

There is, however, a universal five-step progression from first interest or novice to becoming an expert in any field of endeavor. This progression was examined by two brothers, Hubert L. and Stuart E. Dreyfuss (1986), in a book about computers, and by James F. Dalton, Eric T. Jones, and Robert B. Dalton (1990), in a book about the markets. This progression will provide us with a framework for creating our map as we move from one level to another and for studying the historical and scientific differences at each level.

Imagine that you have just attended a piano concert featuring Mozart sonatas. During and after the concert, you have become so uplifted and inspired that you decide, "Whatever it takes, I am going to learn to play the piano. No matter my background, lack of musical talent, age, or whatever—I am going to play the piano!" To parallel this scenario, let's assume that you have been persuaded—by potential profits, challenge, enjoyment, lifestyle, and so on—that you are going to learn the Profitunity approach to trading commodities.

For your music goal, you would most likely buy or rent a piano, buy an instruction manual, and hire a teacher. For your trading goal, you would most likely buy or lease some quote equipment, begin tuning in to CNBC-FNN, subscribe to newsletters, and hire "teachers" in the form of workshops, books, and/or tutorials. In each case, at this level, you are a *novice*.

You are exposed to all sorts of material that will create either good (effective) or bad (losing) habits and concepts. You are very excited and are living on what psychology calls "germination" energy. You feel as though you're entering a new romance. You have an abundance of energy and almost every thought is, "Let's get on with it."

In music, you are learning the basics—the value of a whole note, a half note, a rest, and so on. You learn where middle C is and the correct fingering for playing a scale on the keyboard. You are dealing with individual notes and octaves as opposed to tunes and compositions. In the Profitunity approach, you are learning to trade so that you don't lose money while gaining experience in the market. Let's examine this Level One or novice level.

LEVEL ONE: THE NOVICE

The objectives in music at the novice level are: to learn the rudiments of music notation and to begin to understand the vocabulary and abbreviations on the sheet music. Trading is no different. You are learning to read the language of the market. As each level is introduced in this chapter, look for this highlighting of the objective and tools for that level, using the Profitunity approach to trading.

Novice Level

Objective: To not lose money while gaining experience

Tools: OHLC, volume, MFI, Profitunity windows and air bag

In science, the characteristics of this level are *numbers*. In music, they are the written notes. In computers, they are the binary digits. In physiology, the key is the left hemisphere of the human brain. In history, it is the Middle Ages. In math, it is the level of arithmetic. The assumptions are Aristotelian in that everything is discrete and you can count and/or classify everything in the universe.

At Level One of trading, we are learning the basics of the market: vocabulary, how to put on a trade, what margin requirements mean, and so on. We begin to see the enormous amount of information contained in the tools at this level. These tools are the price bar or OHLC (open, high, low, and close), volume, Market Facilitation Index (MFI), and the Profitunity windows and protective air bag. We are looking at the market on a bar-by-bar process. We are focusing on only two bars, the present bar and the one immediately preceding it. Our primary interest is to understand the evolving behavior of the market rather than to attempt to fit some pattern or "template" from the past onto the current market behavior.

This is the first step on the way to becoming an expert trader. As a novice, you learn how to determine who is running the show and what is currently being done. You begin to identify trends of various lengths. Most novice traders search for a mechanical system that will make them rich and successful if they can just put the pieces of the market puzzle together. Forget it; this will not happen. If you are trading from this perspective, you are doomed as soon as your luck runs out. There simply are not "good mechanical maps" to follow at this level. In my opinion, there never has been a consistently successful "mechanical" system. There isn't now and there most likely never will be, even with artificial intelligence, analog coprocessors, genetic algorithms, orthogonal regression, and neural networks. As you understand how the market really works (remember the Flintstones), you will understand that the market is designed to destroy any successful mechanical system. *All mechanical systems die!* They are linear tools and cannot accurately or adequately describe a nonlinear market. If there *was* a consistently successful mechanical system, it would not be worth $3,000 but could be sold in hours for $30 million. Note that we are talking about a mechanical system that will work consistently and profitably over time.

The maps used by novice traders are generally price comparisons, which all fall short of being adequate because price is an effect and not a cause. They are comparing effect with effect. This technique generally does not lead to profitable trading. Every now and then, it will send out a "good signal," but using these tools does not produce consistent profits. I have laid down this challenge around the world: for every instance where some typical trading signals—divergence, above or below 80 percent, and so on—produced a profit, I can show you five signals of the same type that would have produced losses. I am including stochastics, RSI (Relative Strength Index), momentum, channels, and some other "old reliables."

The function of the novice level is to trade in the market and not lose money while you gain experience. In the typical scenario, most novices, whether in music, romance, or trading, tend to generate an enormous amount of "germination" energy. What follows this elation is usually depression.

"I didn't realize that, to really play the piano well, I need to spend four hours practicing each day for *years*."

"That girl [boy] didn't look quite so good after I learned more about her [his] personality."

"Trading is really a much trickier business than I anticipated. Each time I take a step forward, that seems to be followed by a step backward."

This is the point where most novice traders leave trading. Past statistics indicate that the majority of new traders last just over three months in the market. For those souls who can weather this depression by continuing to practice music or to learn more about trading, there are great rewards in store.

As you practice this microscopic study (we only look at two adjacent bars) of market behavior, you begin to get insights into how the market really works. You begin to realize that it is a product of nature and not of economics, fundamentals, or technicals. Just as skill in bicycle riding comes only after enough falls to teach you the internal principles of balance, so the novice level begins to teach you about the balance of the markets. This then opens the doors of opportunity to enter the next level of understanding, perception, and performance.

LEVEL TWO: THE ADVANCED BEGINNER

At this level, we expand our horizons timewise to include more bars than we examined at Level One. We are now moving from novice to advanced beginner.

Advanced Beginner Level

Objective: To make money consistently on a one-contract basis

Tools: Elliott wave and fractals

The advanced beginner in music has learned the basic notes and chords, has started to put together music that is pleasing to both the player and listeners, and is enjoying the newly acquired skills. Let's look at some of the differences between Level One and Level Two.

Where Level One in math is arithmetic and numbers, Level Two is *space* (geometry). In music at Level One we are concerned with tones; at Level Two, we become concerned with tunes. In computers, Level Two is the analog computer. In history, it is the Renaissance. It is looking at the shadows as well as the leaves. It is moving from one dimension to a higher dimension. Information is available that is not obvious at level one. In the market, some examples of Level Two maps are the fractal and the Elliott wave. The time frame has now changed from comparing two adjacent bars to a more panoramic view of 140 bars or more.

At this point, all traders reach a crucial impasse. Is the motivation for trading strong enough to overcome the temporary frustrations of the market's learning experiences? Just as gravity provides frustrations that help you learn about balance on a bicycle, so will market losses let you learn more about yourself and the balance points of the markets.

Fractals and the Elliott wave are tools that reveal the underlying structure of the market. The Elliott wave provides a directory to the up-and-down moves of the market. The Profitunity approach to analyzing the Elliott wave takes out 90 percent of the ambiguity and gives alternative strategies for dealing with the other 10 percent.

I view trading much like the beginning of a new manufacturing endeavor. The first thing you want is to produce a quality product. If you increase production before you have a quality product, you will face returns from dissatisfied customers. The time to increase production is only after you have a quality product. In the markets, a quality product is being able to make profits consistently on a one-contract basis. If you are not doing this, you either don't have a quality approach to trading or you are not implementing the technique properly.

The advanced beginner has become a quality producer of profits. The next move is to the competent level, where you begin trading on a multiple-contract basis, and the skills learned at Levels One and Two become automatic. A trader's focus at this point is on maximization of the return on investment (ROI) as opposed to profit per contract. Professionally, at this level, a trader is in the top 3 percent of the profession. We are now talking *real* money!

LEVEL THREE: THE COMPETENT TRADER

Competent Level

Objective: To maximize the total ROI by trading multiple contracts, spreads, and writing options

Tools: Profitunity Trading Partner and Profitunity Planned Trading

At this level, a piano student can play *exactly* what is written on the sheet music. Passages that should be loud are played loud; up-tempo parts are played fast. Being competent means following the directions precisely as indicated on the sheet music. In trading, being competent means increasing your total ROI. You are reading the market script accurately. When the market says buy, you buy; when it says sell, you sell; and when it says stay out, you stay out. You are "bringing home the bacon" competently and consistently. In a phrase, you are not getting in the way of your profit-producing tools.

Level Three opens up another type of universe. In history, it is characterized by the Industrial Revolution, when new opportunities and benefits opened up because of new and different understandings about production and economics. In math, this level is characterized by algebra, which allows us to look for and solve problems with unknown quantities. It permits the finding of x, the "unknown" factor. It is the early beginnings of understanding chaos. Level Three begins to monitor what most people call "causes" rather than just effects.

The tools of the market at this level include Profitunity Planned Trading™, which allows maximum flexibility and profit from monitoring the underlying and unseen structure of the market. It allows one to get into the "rhythm" and to start "dancing" to the tune the market is currently playing. It also allows one to know whether an analysis is "wrong" or "out of touch" with the market. If wrong, the appropriate strategy is to stop and reverse. If "out of touch," the best strategy is to get out.

The purpose of Profitunity Planned Trading is to squeeze the maximum amount of profits for a specified move, letting the market (rather than some arbitrary system) determine the most appropriate strategy. Profitunity Planned Trading provides the most profit/least risk formula for asset allocation.

The other primary tool at this level is the Profitunity Trading Partner™. The purpose of the Profitunity Trading Partner is to consider and prioritize opportunities and affix the most appropriate measures to protect the trader's investment. Experienced use of the Profitunity Trading Partner allows one to do a complete analysis on any chart and know, in 10 seconds or less, what one should do on every bar: buy, sell, pyramid, stop and reverse, or just get out. At Level Three, you learn the tremendous advantage of being able to make an "instant and correct" assessment of any market.

You no longer spend hours each day analyzing the market. Most traders spend so much time in analysis they miss most of the opportunities the market offers daily.

Once you reach Level Three, you are a self-sufficient professional trader. You are acquainted with the always underlying and usually unseen structure of the markets. You no longer need or desire outside opinions. You don't need to read *The Wall Street Journal,* listen to CNBC-FNN, subscribe to newsletters, or waste money on hotlines. However, this is only half of the equation. The other half is the trader as a person.

There are thousands and maybe hundreds of thousands of musicians who are much more competent than Frank Sinatra, yet more of his records have been sold than anyone else's on earth. In live concert, he is often flat, and his timing is his own doing. But the difference that sells records and makes him profits is that he does *not* sing a song exactly the way it was written. He adds and communicates *feeling*. The largest leap in the entire five-step progression from novice to expert is be-tween Level Three and Level Four. At Level Four, you have an "educated intuition" or a "gut feeling" about the market that is usually very accurate. You are manipulating your own struc-ture to correspond with the market's structure. At Level Four, winning becomes the path of least resistance.

LEVEL FOUR: THE PROFICIENT TRADER

Proficient Level

Objective: To trade your own belief systems

Tools: Left hemisphere, core, right hemisphere (brain wiring)

At this level, a musician's prime objective is to be able to com-municate feelings through the language of music. Feelings are translated, through a pianist's fingers, to the piano keys, which make sound waves that move listeners' emotions. In trading, you are trading your belief systems (aligning your un-derlying structure with that of the market), and your enjoy-ment comes not only from making profits but also from the satisfaction of feeling your trading is in sync with the market.

Level Four is a quantum leap beyond the three lower levels. In history, it is the electronic revolution that allows us to bring in much more powerful data processors than ever before

71

available to humans. Stability we formerly counted on changes at an ever-increasing rate. My 486 computer, my tool for writing this book, has more manipulating power than everything available to the entire world in the past century. Think about it: from this single keyboard, I have more computing power than the entire world had only 100 years ago. To give you an idea of what is happening at an ever-increasing rate, let's go back to 1975. At that time, a Rolls Royce sedan cost $65,000. Computing power at that time was much more expensive than it is now. If Rolls Royce had reduced the ticket price of a sedan as much as the price of computing power has been reduced, the same model Rolls purchased new today would cost 30 cents. We now have the power, at very little expense, to look at infinitely large masses of data and infinitely small particles and divisions. This puts power into the budget of every trader. The complexity of chaos, which has been anathema to progress, is now becoming available everywhere. In math, this level is calculus, which allows us to "differentiate" to micro infinity on the one hand and to "integrate" to macro infinity on the other.

Traders also make a quantum leap to this level. They begin to see that they are a vital part of this whole process, and they bring to the equation all of their background, philosophy, and belief systems. At this level, traders make use of the fact that no one trades the markets, they trade their own individual belief systems. Just as the computer revolution has allowed us to see inside the masses of data and to make sense of them, the new science of chaos is allowing us to look into our behavior with a focus not available to the Aristotelian, Euclidean, Newtonian, and classical physics/psychology approaches.

At this level, we begin to understand and work with our own personal body type and our individual brain structure. The Profitunity Trading Group has developed this understanding to a new level of precision. Our objective is to align our own personal underlying structure with the underlying structure of the market. Let me restate that when that happens, winning becomes the path of least resistance.

LEVEL FIVE: THE EXPERT TRADER

Expert Level

Objective: To trade your states of mind

Tools: Your own various states of mind (biological software)

This is the beckoning point that invites us into realms of understanding we have only dreamed of until now. At Level Five, we see that basically everything is information, and our purpose in dealing with this information is to *find out who we are.* At this level, trading truly becomes a "game" in the largest and best sense of that word; everything is important and everything is a teacher. We understand ourselves and the market, and that understanding gives us more control over both.

At Level Five, we flow deeply into the realm of **chaos.** In sports, this realm is sometimes called the "zone." Chaos does not mean "disorder"; rather, it is a higher form of order that becomes all-inclusive. There is no randomness. What we call random at Levels One through Three is really a catchall for our lack of insight and understanding.

At this level, trading is a low-stress way of living. You feel as though you are floating down a river that is providing you with any desire you name. Your nice fantasy has become completely achievable by following the Profitunity approach.

SUMMARY

In this chapter, we have looked at the five steps that will take you from being a novice trader to being an expert, and at the parameters that will indicate the level where you are currently trading. We have also listed the objectives and tools that are appropriate at each level. For quick reference, they are tabulated as follows:

Level	Objective	Tools
1. Novice	To not lose money while gaining experience	OHLC, volume, MFI, Profitunity windows and air bag
2. Advanced beginner	To make money consistently on a one-contract basis	Elliott wave and fractals
3. Competent	To maximize the total ROI	Profitunity Trading Partner and Profitunity Planned Trading
4. Proficient	To trade your own belief systems	Left hemisphere, core, right hemisphere (brain wiring)
5. Expert	To trade your states of mind	Your own various states of mind (biological software)

In the next chapter, we examine in detail Level One, the first step of the journey to becoming an expert trader. We will study all the Level One tools and delineate exactly what type of feedback to monitor.

——— 6 ———

Level One: Novice Trader

Nature's way is simple and easy, but men prefer the intricate and artificial.

Lao Tzu

GOAL: TO START READING THE MARKET ITSELF RATHER THAN READING OTHER PEOPLE'S OPINIONS ABOUT THE MARKET

In this chapter, we will look at the fundamentals that are necessary to begin understanding and trading the markets. The best way to approach this material is to consider each item and each decision as a learning experience. As mentioned in the previous chapter, there is a great deal of excitement in starting a new adventure. We labeled this "germination" energy. Your market adventure will be different from all others. I tell my seminars that trading is the most "naked psychotherapy" in the world. It is an incredible "learning about yourself" experience. Commodity trading can not only add cash to your account but will put excitement, fun, and understanding into your life.

New traders typically want more information than they have available when they take a position. Recall our Flintstone market and realize that if you had all the indicators in the

75

world and all the information in the world you would be absolutely 100 percent ambivalent. The market features an equal division between buying pressure and selling pressure, so *more* information is not the answer. The answer is the right information in the right form. In this chapter, we begin devising an approach that will take the overwhelming amount of information the market puts out each minute and funnel it down into a form and language that will make your trading decisions easy. We will end up with a simple, unambivalent, decision-based language.

Specifically, you will learn who is running this show called the market—who the people in charge are and, more importantly, what they are doing. You will also learn how to determine which way the market is going (note the present tense). In the next chapter, you will learn how to anticipate, with considerable accuracy, which way the market will go in the future.

You will learn one of the most significant advances in market analysis in the past 30 years. This is an original indicator that is used throughout the world. By the time you have finished this chapter, you will know more about the real market than 90 percent of all the traders currently in the market.

The goal at Level One of Profitunity trading is to not lose money while gaining experience in trading the market. This goal should be achievable with the material in this chapter.

The markets are so unimaginably large that neither the enormously rich Hunt brothers nor George Soros could corner even one small part of them. Central bank intervention from the largest countries in the world can only affect the market over a very short time. The first thing we must give up, in order to trade profitably, is any idea that we can affect the market. Our only choice is to follow, and we want to be sure we're following the market movers.

When I said you would learn who is running the show, I was referring to the traders that are trading the largest number of contracts. Knowing their actual identity is not important.

What they are doing—buying and selling large-volume orders—is of the utmost importance, and understanding their choices and actions is not as difficult to determine as most traders think.

Let's start with the basic unit of commodity trading—one bar on a market chart. The information that the market gives us is the OHLC (Figure 6–1), or open, high, low, and close (all moments of price), the volume, and the time. Most traders do not realize the enormous amount of information contained in those numbers. The key is understanding the relationship between the open and close when compared to the high and the low of the present bar.

The open tells us where the balance point between buyers and sellers was at the opening of a period, regardless of the time period we are discussing. We follow market action by examining the movement of the balance point throughout this time period.

The high tells us the highest point to which the bulls' combined action moved the price. The bulls obviously want the price to go higher than the top of the bar, to let them make more profit. There is always that counter-balancing point where the bulls run out of steam and/or the bears become strong enough to stop the advance. This is to the bears' advantage and desire because they are losing money on every tick of a climbing market.

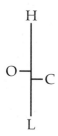

Figure 6–1 Open, high, low, and close (single bar).

The low tells us the exact price at which the bears ran out of steam and the bulls rejected their downward momentum.

The close tells us where that all-essential balance point was at the end of the period. If the period has a longer time frame (day, week, month), the close also tells us where the trading population was balanced to leave the price overnight, over a weekend, and so on.

The above four prices tell us much vital information, but even more important is the movement of that balance point. There is a need for some systematic way to measure and tabulate the possible varieties of movement patterns and the meanings they have for us as traders.

We have found that the most convenient, easiest, and most profitable approach is to divide the current bar into thirds and to number the three equal sections from top to bottom, as shown in Figure 6–2.

Next, we want an easy method to identify what is happening during a particular time period. We need some sort of translation device that will condense the pertinent market information into a language or code that will make the decision-making process simple, fast, easy, obvious, and overall profitable.

The Profitunity approach, after dividing the bar into equal thirds, identifies both the open and the close in relation to the high and low achieved by the current bar. We arbitrarily give

Figure 6–2 Bar divided into thirds.

the open the first number and the close the second number. The number assigned to the open and close is determined by the segment of the bar (top, middle, or bottom) in which the open and close occurred. Figure 6–3 is an example of two bars. For the first bar, the open and close occurred in the top third, the segment numbered 1. The bar on the left is then referred to as a 1-1 bar. The bar on the right is labeled a 3-3 bar because both the open and close occurred in the bottom third of that bar. Whenever you see an extreme (a bar that both opens and closes in the same third, top or bottom, of the bar), *85% of the time the market will change direction within the next 1 to 5 bars* of the same duration as the bar you are examining. This knowledge alone can change the results of your trading. It is extremely helpful for intraday trading.

Psychologically, the two bars in Figure 6–3 represent an "approach–avoidance" type of behavior: they open, start in one direction, and come back to near where they started. The result is little directional price movement from the open to the close. There is even more valuable information to glean from this one bar. It tells us exactly who was in charge and what they were doing during different parts of this time period. For example, in the 1-1 bar (both open and close were in the top third), we know that in the early part of the period the bears were in charge and that during the latter part of the period the bulls were in charge. But wait (as they say in TV infomercials),

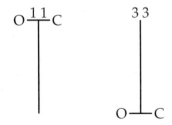

Figure 6–3   A 1–1 bar and a 3–3 bar.

79

there's more. We also know who was in charge at the end of the period. The *buyers* were. Why? Because the bar closed in the top third. There simply cannot be any other explanation of the trading behavior during that bar.

The opposite information is true for the 3-3 bar. The buyers were in charge during the early part of the period, and the sellers were in charge during the latter part of the period and remained in charge at the end of the period. All that information is contained in every bar on whatever chart you look at. At this point we are using a microscope to examine the information. Later, we'll use a wide-angle lens to see the broader pictures the market can capture. The charts are like paint-by-numbers pictures. Small areas of uniform colors appear first, and shortly a larger image starts to emerge and you can identify what the artist (the market) is communicating.

In contrast to the 1-1 or 3-3 bar, we have a 2-2 bar (Figure 6–4), which leaves us with considerably more ambiguity than the extremes. It is labeled a 2-2 bar because both the open and the close occurred in the middle third of the bar. Unlike the extreme bars, it does not tell us for sure who is in charge at the close of the period. To indicate that it gives us relatively little information, we label this bar a *neutral*. In candlestick terminology, this would be known either as a spinning top or a doji. The 2-2 bar indicates that neither the buyers nor the sellers were in overwhelming control during this period.

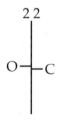

Figure 6–4   A 2–2 bar.

In this particular paradigm of bar arrangements, there are only nine possible alternatives. We have already covered three of them (2 extremes and 1 neutral). This next group we call *climbers.* Their common characteristic is that the open is always lower than the close. Their labels are 3-1, 2-1, and 3-2, as shown in Figure 6–5.

The 3-1 bar gives us the greatest amount of information: it tells us that the buyers were in control during the entire period. In market profile terms, this could be a trend day. The 2-1 bar gives us a bit less information but does tell us that the buyers were in control at the end of the period. The 3-2 bar gives us the least amount of information of all the climbers. It tells us that the buyers were able to make the close higher than the open but, at some time during the bar period, the sellers took the price below the high. And we cannot be certain who was in charge at the end of this period.

In the last group of three different possibilities, labeled *drifters,* the close is lower than the open and the price is coming down. The group includes the 1-2, 2-3, and the 1-3 bars (Figure 6–6).

The 1-3 bar gives us the most information: the sellers were basically in charge throughout the period and certainly were still in charge at the end of the period. The 2-3 bar gives us a bit less information, but it does indicate that the sellers were in charge at the end of the period. The 1-2 bar gives us the least

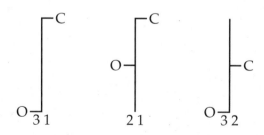

Figure 6–5   Climbers: 3–1, 2–1, and 3–2.

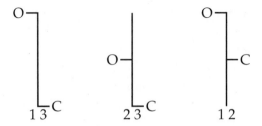

Figure 6–6   Drifters: 1–3, 2–3, and 1–2.

amount of information. We cannot be certain that either buyers or sellers were in charge at the end of the period.

We know now that, by looking at the open, high, low, and close of a bar, we are able to tell a great deal about who is in charge and what they are doing. The important concept to grasp is that each bar clearly indicates how the interaction between buyers and sellers moved the balance point around during the period. This information alone is more than the majority of traders can read into the market.

LONGER-TERM MOVEMENT

We need a second data input to narrow down our evaluation of market action: Which way is the immediate trend? By *immediate*, I mean compared to the previous bar of the same length. For example, on a 5-minute bar, we are talking about a total of 10 minutes (2 bars). On a 1-hour bar, we are looking at a total of 2 hours.

Our "quick and dirty" way to determine the trend is shown in the pairs of bars in Figure 6–7. If the midpoint of the current bar is above the top of the most recent bar, the trend is up and is indicated with a plus sign (+). If the midpoint is inside the range of the previous bar, we designate it with "O" and call it an overlap with no clear trend. If the midpoint is below the

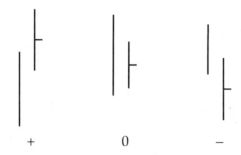

Figure 6–7   Determining the immediate trend.

range of the previous bar, we mark it with a minus sign (−) to indicate the trend is down.

Now we know who is in charge and what they are doing, and we begin to get a feel for the longer-term picture by knowing which way the immediate trend is going. Our next task is to look deeper into what is actually happening during the trading day (or any longer time period). What are the various interacting forces that determine price, price movement, and the termination of a price move (the end of a trend)?

Trends

A rather old axiom of trading is that the best way to make profits consistently in trading is by following the trends. A source of real confusion is that the other axiom of making money in the market is: "Buy low and sell high." As mentioned in Chapter 2, these two axioms are obviously contradictory. If you buy low and sell high, you are going directly *against* the trend. The ideal, of course, is to buy low at the very beginning of a new upward trend. To develop this ability, let's look at how trends are formed.

Years ago, the "market" and the "marketplace" occupied the same physical space. Most of the large grain commercials were on the trading floor. Their orders were of sufficient size to move the market, and they had much more control over the market than they do today. During the past 20 years, the markets have become worldwide. Not only are Ralston Purina, Kellogg, and other large commercials trying to hedge their bets, but millions more small speculators and farmers all over the world are competing with them in anticipating the future prices of grain. This spells great opportunity for traders. Today, trends are *not* made on the floor. The floor primarily provides a liquid market by responding to "outside" orders.

The fact that trends are now made off the floor, rather than on the floor as they were previously, gives us an opportunity to anticipate what the market is going to do. The key is *volume*. Our only real-time information from this market is tick volume, time, and price. Tick volume is the number of price changes made during a specified period. It is not the number of contracts traded. A number of studies have indicated that there is no significant difference between the relationship of actual volume and tick volume. We use tick volume and can assume that it represents actual volume. This on-line volume is our best clue to what is happening in the trading pits.

In the pits are two basic species: floor brokers and locals. Floor brokers are the people who fill orders. They get paid a salary, a commission, or some combination of those two factors. Generally, they do not have their own money on the line. They are order fillers. Their financial future is not affected directly by the prices they get for orders filled.

Locals trade with their own money. If they don't get good prices, they pay out of their pockets then and there. Locals must be much better traders than floor brokers. Locals must make their own decisions; floor brokers generally follow someone else's orders. Locals' primary function is to make a market by taking the other side of a trade. They usually are not interested in any long-term positions. We have had dozens of locals at our private tutorials, and to some of them a 10-minute trade can be a long-term position. Remember that trends are made from orders off the floor rather than from the locals' taking longer-term positions. Because the locals' main job is to take the other side of outside orders, they have no future in trading with each other. They are after *your* money. Again, our key to understanding the action in the pit is tick volume. The locals do no significant amount of trading with other locals, and trends are made by outside paper. We must know, therefore, when and in what amounts outside paper is coming to the floor. This is signaled by a *change in tick volume.*

The bar chart in Figure 6–8 has a tick volume histogram on the bottom. Compare any bar with the immediately preceding bar. If the present bar (the right-hand bar in the pair) has more volume than the previous one, more outside orders are coming to the floor. Before a trend can start, there must be more volume coming to the floor. An increase in volume always precedes an increase in momentum, and the momentum changes

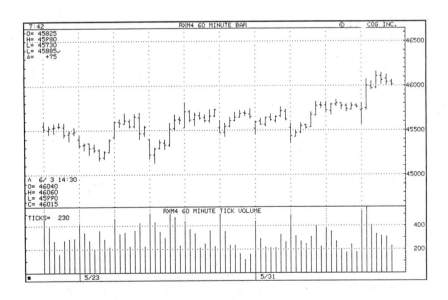

Figure 6–8   Price chart with tick volume in lower chart.

before the trend changes. Before any of this starts, hundreds or even thousands of decisions must be made by outside traders who are changing their minds about the market. Let's restate this sequence for clarity. The first changes are the decisions in traders' minds off the floor. Their decisions are then reflected in changes in tick volume. After that comes a change in momentum, and then, finally, a change in trend. Our goal is to get in on the first 10 percent of any change in trend, and get out on the final 10 percent of that same trend. If you can do this, you will be rich. Again, for emphasis, the first key is a *change in tick volume.*

A practical rule in intraday trading is: A difference of one tick is enough. We are interested in whether there is more or less volume than in the previous time period. If we are trading on a daily chart, we use ±10 percent as a significant difference in volume. Trading dailies, we must have 110 percent of the previous day's volume to be counted a plus (+). Volume that is 90 percent or less would count as a minus (−), and between 91 percent and 109 percent would count as the same volume. Our task here is to take all the complicated information the markets are giving out each second and translate or funnel it into an easy-to-understand decision format. The only language the market speaks is *ticks, volume,* and *time.* Let's examine more closely the syntax of this language.

THE MARKET FACILITATION INDEX

Whenever the tick volume goes up, we know we have more outside paper coming in; whenever it goes down, we know that less outside paper is coming to the floor. Our next task is to assess accurately the effect this change in volume has on the market. It is not enough to know how much; it is more important to know how the market reacts to this change in volume. Heavier volume does not always mean the market will move. The market's main task is to find a *balance point,* and it will do it in a fraction of a second. That balance point will only move when there is a bias of incoming orders, so we need a *bias finder.*

This bias finder works in both trending and bracketed (range-bound) markets. It is relatively easy to make profits in a trend. The problem is keeping those profits when there is not a trend. Many experienced traders will tell you that it is easy to make money trading but hard to keep it. The profits made in a trend are swept back during bracketed markets. We worked on this task for over five years before developing a simple and accurate measure to make trading more profitable. In 1983, when we started developing this indicator, we felt that when the markets were in a bracket, trading was like slogging through mud; when they were trending, it was as if they were running on concrete. So, we first referred to this indicator as the *mud factor:* the more mud, the slower the market would move. About 1986, we started calling it *tic mileage* because we were measuring the mileage in terms of *price change per tick.* In 1989, we became more sophisticated and started calling it the Market Facilitation Index (MFI). This index is now used worldwide and comes as a standard indicator on several technical analysis systems.

The MFI is very simple. Determine the range of whatever time period you are observing by subtracting the low from the high. Then divide that number by the volume. Expressed as a formula:

$$\text{MFI} = \frac{\text{Range (High} - \text{Low)}}{\text{Volume}}$$

Breaking this formula down, you can see that it is measuring the change in price per tick:

$$\frac{\text{Range}}{\text{Volume}} = \frac{\Delta \text{ Price}}{\text{Tick}}$$

Comparing this to Einstein's formula $E = mc^2$, we can solve for the constant c^2 by transposing the m (mass):

$$c^2 = \frac{E}{m} = \frac{Range}{Volume}$$

In trading, the mass would correspond to volume, and the energy would correspond to the price movement. Would Einstein agree? I have no idea, but it's fun to speculate, in trading and thinking.

We are measuring the effective change in price per tick. This number has *no absolute value.* Its value lies in comparing this number with a previous MFI. For example, if the current bar's MFI = .541, that is not comparable in any way with a bar from yesterday's chart that might have a value of .541. We are interested in the MFI in relation to the immediate previous market action. We want to know whether there is more or less market facilitation of price movement. The MFI is a measure of the market's willingness to move the price. I cannot overemphasize the value of this indicator. It is a more truthful measure of market action than any stochastic, RSI (Relative Strength Index) or other momentum indicator. Whatever you do, don't insult it by comparing it to someone's analysis or forecast. *This is where the truth of the market is found.*

The MFI's measurement of how many points the market traveled per tick is an extremely accurate description of the efficiency of the market during this particular bar. If the current MFI is greater than the previous MFI, we observe more price movement per tick and greater facilitation of price movement through time. Again, we are comparing only the current bar's MFI with the immediately preceding bar's MFI. This allows us to determine whether the present time period is providing more or fewer trading opportunities.

A tremendous advantage of the Profitunity approach is that *nothing is optimized.* The MFI continually changes on a relative basis within the market's current volatility. Thus, as the market's personality changes over time, so will the MFI and its various relationships.

Let's sum up what we've learned at this first stage (novice level) of understanding the market and its opportunities. We know how to determine:

1. Who is moving the market (buyers or sellers);

2. Which direction the market is moving;

3. What kind of job the market is doing in facilitation price movement through time (MFI).

All of these information items, by constantly interacting with each other, will reveal various market conditions and different trading opportunities.

Next, we can combine the above factors to increase the power of our understanding and our analysis of market action.

The MFI/Volume Combination

A change in volume alerts us before a trend begins, and the MFI reveals how the market is reacting to this increase/decrease in volume. By combining these two factors, we can get a more vivid and accurate picture of market action. We will use volume twice, but in different ways: (1) we use raw volume as revealed by tick volume, and (2) we use volume in computing the MFI. After using the MFI for a very short while, you will recognize visually whether the MFI is greater or less. Don't get bogged down thinking you have to use the calculator on every bar. You can also obtain several computer programs to color the bars, depending on changes in the MFI. Remember that we are *uncomplicating* the market action for easy, accurate, and quick decisions. In our tutorials, we have a goal that after four days of training you should be able to analyze a chart you have never seen before (one that contains roughly 140 bars; a day chart will cover over 6 months of action) and know what your position (long or short) should be on each bar, where your stops should be, where you should pyramid, and where to take profits—and do all of this in *10 seconds or less.* Over decades, I spent 5 to 9 hours per day analyzing the markets. Now, using the exact procedure I describe in this chapter, I follow over 30 markets and need less than 20 minutes of analysis time per day for *all the markets combined.*

In the rest of this chapter, I introduce some helpful tools and show you how to use them effectively.

THE PROFITUNITY WINDOWS

Profitunity windows are more than just windows of opportunity. By combining the two factors—volume and MFI—in all four possible combinations, your odds for success become so much better that we call them profitunities rather than opportunities.

I have assigned an indicator to each of the possible combinations, to describe exactly what is happening in both the broad market and the reactions in the pits. We'll look at them one by one. This tabulation will be a handy reference to the four combinations:

Tick Volume/MFI Combinations	Indicator	
1. + Tick volume and + MFI	Green	(+ +)
2. − Tick volume and − MFI	Fade	(− −)
3. − Tick volume and + MFI	Fake	(− +)
4. + Tick volume and − MFI	Squat	(+ −)

Green (+ Tick Volume and + MFI)

We label this bar a "green" because it is a green light for market movement. Movement is already happening. Pretend that you are a hobo in an east coast freight yard, looking for a train going west. You have two different ways to find the right train. First, you could wander around the freight yard in search of a train whose waybills are all for western states, on the premise that such a train will eventually be going west. When you find one, you could board a nice box car, make yourself comfortable, and wait for the engine to hook up and go. Your second choice might be to stand on the western end of the freight yard and jump onto the first train coming out of the yard on the westbound tracks. The second choice would be a "green." The train is already on the move. Like the moving train coming out of the yard, a green may be dangerous to tag onto. You certainly would not want to stand in front of it, which is exactly what you would be doing if you tried to trade against the direction of a green bar.

A green is a breakout signal and your best immediate strategy is to *go with* whatever direction it is going. A green signifies three things:

1. More players are entering the market (+ volume);

2. The arriving players are biased in the direction the bar is moving;

3. The price movement is picking up speed as it goes (+ MFI).

Fade (− Tick Volume and − MFI)

A "fade" occurs when the market is taking a breath or losing interest. A fade is the opposite of a green: both volume and MFI (price movement) are less. The futures market is an auction market, and the bidders are losing interest. If I were auctioning this computer I am writing on, many people would instantly offer me $100 for it. With that kind of response, I would raise the price. Considerably fewer bidders would offer me $1,000 for it, and I am sure no one would offer $5,000. As the price goes up, more and more bidders lose interest. This is what a fade indicates. Often, the top of the first wave in an Elliott wave sequence has a fade top: not a lot of action, and the excitement of the market is dwindling. It is very important to point out that fade areas (we are illustrating these concepts with just two bars, but the same reasoning applies to areas of multiple bars; more about that later) are the start of big moves. So the very time when the market is most boring is exactly the time when a good trader must be on guard for any sign that momentum is building.

Fake (− Tick Volume and + MFI)

With a "fake," we have a situation where the MFI is increasing, which means the market is facilitating itself by moving price through time but is not supported by increasing volume from outside the pit. Therefore, the facilitation is less robust, as indicated by the *decrease* in raw volume. For whatever reasons, the market is attracting less volume than in the previous period. A fake sometimes indicates a pause in the market action before the market "takes off." Unless this situation is followed shortly by increasing volume, the fake has probably been manipulated by the locals in the pit. The locals are in temporary control simply because no significant volume of outside paper is coming into the pit. The fake is a trademark of pit manipulation and should be viewed with a high degree of skepticism.

The locals have sensed that a move is imminent during the lull in the pit action. This is the only time when the locals have enough power to "run your stops." They will, if possible, take the market in the opposite direction of the anticipated move, in order to acquire inventory and take the other side of the anticipated paper coming into the pit. They are building their inventory so they can sell the next rally or buy the next decline.

Squat (+ Tick Volume and − MFI)

A "squat" is the strongest potential money maker of the four Profitunity windows. Virtually all moves end with a squat as the high/low bar plus or minus one bar of the same time period. Another way of stating this is that all significant trends end with a squat on one of the three top or bottom bars. This analysis provides a potentially effective way to get in on the beginning of a trend. While all trends end in a squat, all squats are not the end of a trend. Squats appear quite often in the middle of Elliott wave 3 and at Fibonacci retracements and Gann line intersections (see Chapter 7). If it does not end the immediate trend, it tends to become a "measuring squat" (similar to a measuring gap) predicting how far the current move will continue. This measuring squat gives us a target zone where we can look for another squat that may end the current trend.

Squats are characterized by a greater tick volume and a lower MFI, and, usually but not always, by a smaller range than the previous bar. If you are trading short-term charts (intraday), a visual shorthand for a squat would be the same or a smaller range with a higher tick volume (compared to the previous bar).

The squat is the last battle of the bears and the bulls, with lots of buying and selling but little price movement. There is an almost equal division between the number and enthusiasm of both bears and bulls. A real war is taking place and the equivalent of hand-to-hand combat is going on in the pits. I labeled this a squat because it appears that the market is squatting, getting ready to leap one way or the other (often, in a reversal of the current trend). The market has moved up or down on substantial volume, and now a flood of sellers or buyers enters the market. Volume increases, the trend is stalled, and the price movement virtually stops. The key is that the price movement stops on higher volume. One of the two opposing forces (buyers vs. sellers) will win, and usually the breakout of the squat will let you know whether this squat is a trend continuation or a trend reversal squat.

THE AIR BAG: PROTECTION
AGAINST DISASTER

I have been driving a car for over 45 years and have never been in an accident that I have caused. From that history, you might conclude that I am or at least have been a careful driver and need limited protection from my own driving. During that same 45 years, I have been through the windshield twice in head-on collisions. In both cases, I was sitting in the right-front passenger seat and the driver had the car in the proper lane, at a speed that was lower than the limit. Both accidents were caused by drunken drivers going in the opposite direction in the wrong lane.

From these experiences, I would never consider buying a car that did not have dual air bags. Looking at my automobile background statistically, I don't need an air bag for my driving but rather for protection against drunken drivers. Sometimes the market acts like a drunken driver, and you need the protection of an air bag.

As further evidence of the need for an air bag for the market, we know that traders who have exited the market because they could not trade profitably have usually left because of a few big losses rather than many small losses. If you protect your trades carefully, you may have a long string of small losses without having to leave trading. We need an air bag to protect us against large losses.

Fortunately, the market gives us an excellent technique for placing life- and trade-saving losses. The market can be broken down into five different trading time frames that have a similar and constant relationship with each other. We start with the monthly time frame:

Each *month* contains

4.3 *weeks;* each week contains

5 *days;* each day contains

5–6 *trading hours;* each trading hour contains

4 (15-*minute*) or 6 (10-*minute*) bars

Each time frame breaks down to approximately one-fifth of the next higher time frame and approximately five times the next lower time frame.

We place the air bag one tick above/below the high/low of the second bar back on one significantly higher time frame (or the next bar further back that has both a higher high and a higher low or a lower high and a lower low). (See Figure 6–9.)

This is our air bag protection. Its purpose is to protect us against a drunken market that is moving against us. Remember, it is not necessarily an entry signal; it is protection against major losses. If your air bag is a high, it is telling you that you do not want to be short if the market reaches that number. If your air bag is a low, it is telling you that you do not want to be long if the market goes down to that number.

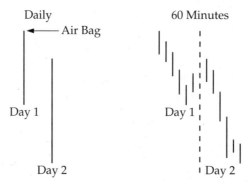

Figure 6–9   Using two different time periods to plan air bag protection.

The vast majority of times, you will get a reversal or an entry signal before the market reaches your air bag. It is there to keep you from making a catastrophic mistake by staying in the market too long.

PUTTING IT TOGETHER AT LEVEL ONE

We now have the elements that can take us from ground zero—a losing trader—toward the first level of consistent profits. When you understand this chapter, you will know more about making profits in the market than 90 percent of all the traders do. You will understand that volume controls the market movements and that trends come from off the floor. All our markets are now basically worldwide markets and will be even more so in the future.

You have the basic tools to translate market action into easily understandable terms and funnel the enormous amounts of information the market gives off each minute into a manageable and concise formula for both analyzing the market and making good trading decisions. You also know how to analyze the incoming volume and how to use the most accurate evaluation of the market's reaction to that volume, the MFI. You know that by combining the raw tick volume and the MFI you have an even better and more sophisticated instrument for understanding exactly what the market is doing and what the likely next move will be.

For example, if the particular bar you are examining opened in the top third and closed in the bottom third (its internal designation of 13 makes it a drifter and tells us exactly what happened during that time period), the market is moving down. If the midpoint of the current bar is above the range of the previous bar, we designate the immediate trend as a minus (−). If we have increasing tick volume compared to the previous bar, which gives volume a plus (+), and the MFI (range divided by ticks) is less than the previous bar, which gives the MFI a minus (−), we would have the following designation:

$$-13+-$$

From this designation, we know that the trend is down, the sellers are in charge throughout this time period, they continue to be in charge at the end of the period, and the Profitunity window is a squat. Ideally, we should be ready to reverse and go long. (See Figure 6–10.)

On the other hand, we could have a somewhat similar configuration with different probabilities. Let's say the trend is up (+), the current bar opened in the bottom third and closed in the top third (31), and we have increasing tick volume (+) and more MFI than for the previous bar (+). Our description of this bar would be +31++ (Figure 6–10). The important difference

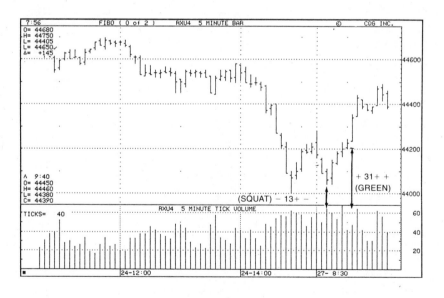

Figure 6–10   A + 13 + − squat bar and a + 31 + + green bar.

97

between this and the prior example is that buyers were in charge throughout this bar and the Profitunity window is a green. Ideally, we should already be on board on the long side, especially since we had a squat bar five bars previous to the current green. This is a "go-with" bar, and we want to stay with it until the market tells us otherwise.

SUMMARY

Our purpose at this novice level is to trade the market without losing money and while gaining valuable experience. If you are not breaking even in your trading, you are not at this level. Even if you are losing, you should continue to read the rest of this book. Look especially at Chapter 10, where we begin using the Profitunity Trading Partner. That aid will improve your trading at any level.

The tools you should now be using are the individual bar analyses (OHLC: open, high, low, and close), which will tell you who is in charge and what they are doing. You should be familiar with information coming from the extreme, neutral, climber, and drifter bars.

You should recognize quickly and easily the immediate trend direction.

You should thoroughly understand the MFI (Market Facilitation Index) and how to combine the MFI with raw volume to produce the Profitunity windows, which offer insight that was not available before. You now know that any bar with increasing volume (compared to the preceding bar) must be either a green or a squat. Either one should wave a flag in your mind, telling you to examine the market closely for any trading opportunities.

Decreasing volume means you will have either a fade or a fake bar. Fades and fakes are much less important than greens and squats, but they alert us to pay attention because big moves most often come from dull markets.

In the next chapter, we move from not losing money to making profits on a consistent basis. From a focus on only two consecutive bars, we will change to a wide-angle view consisting of a minimum of 100 bars. We will continue to use everything learned at Level One in the new, broader, and more profitable Level Two.

The following questions are for your review. Before moving to Level Two trading, you should be able to answer them easily. If some of them still stump you, I suggest you reread the chapter or the relevant sections.

REVIEW QUESTIONS

1. How can you tell who is in charge during a given specific time period?

2. In our bar identification code, which number is the open? Which is the close?

3. What are the two extreme bars, and what information do they give us about the continuation of the present trend?

4. What information does a neutral bar give us?

5. Which of the three climbers gives us the most information about the current market and which gives us the least?

6. Which of the three drifters gives us the most information about the current market and which gives us the least?

7. Where are trends made and how can you identify them?

8. Explain clearly why the MFI is so valuable to profitable trading.

9. Define and describe the four Profitunity windows.

10. Which two Profitunity windows are accompanied by increasing volume?

11. Which of the four Profitunity windows is the most valuable to you as a trader? Why? Where do windows of this type occur?

7

Level Two:
The Advanced Beginner

GOALS:

1. **TO UNDERSTAND THE CONNECTION BETWEEN THE MFI AND ELLIOTT WAVE COUNTING.**
2. **TO USE THE PROFITUNITY MACD TO TAKE THE AMBIGUITY OUT OF ELLIOTT WAVE COUNTING.**

We pointed out earlier that germination energy always follows entry into a new experience. Once they discover that more is involved than they had first envisioned, most new traders become discouraged and never achieve what is there just for the taking. At Level Two, you approach this most critical juncture. Will you become discouraged and decide that no one really makes money trading the markets? Or will you hang in and gain all the benefits of being in the top 1 to 2 percent? At this point in our journey from Level One (novice) to Level Five (expert), we get acquainted with some powerful trading tools. Once these specific tools are mastered, your trading confidence will grow. We will be looking specifically at the underlying structure of the market, which we first discussed in Chapter 4.

At Level One, the novice level, our purpose is to stay in the market and not lose money while gaining experience. At Level Two, the advanced beginner level, we should be taking money from the market on a consistent basis. Level One is concerned with only two bars (on any time frame). We analyze the current bar by looking at the open, high, low, and close. At Level Two, we expand our horizon. While analyzing the Elliott wave, we *must* have a minimum of 100 bars and a maximum of 140 bars. When using the Profitunity Planned Trading approach, we can have virtually any number of bars.

First, we will take apart the Elliott wave. Then we will journey to the far reaches of market analysis and look at the underlying structure of the Elliott wave. This underlying structure comes from the new science of chaos and, specifically, from the fractal of the Elliott wave. After looking at the Elliott wave, we will simplify the trading of it in real time. You have probably heard the saying that if you take two Elliotticians and put them in a room with one chart, they will come out with nine different counts. Not so when you trade with the Profitunity approach.

Almost any issue of a commodity trading magazine will have either a letter or an article about how the Elliott wave is simply too subjective to be of any trading value. Trash that thought! I challenge any trader to come into my trading room and trade with us for just one day. That trader will leave a believer! I have worked with several hundred traders privately, teaching them our approaches to using this tool. As far as I know, I don't have a single disbeliever.

The basic problem is that few traders understand and know how to test where we are in the current count. Any Elliottician can give you a good wave count *after* the fact. Traders need a *current* wave count that is dependable and accurate. That exact tool can be found in Level Two. Following a simple theoretical explanation, we will work through some actual trading examples. In Level Three, we will combine our other proprietary indicators with our fractal analysis to yield the most surefire, least-risk trading possible.

One of the few things that all traders agree on is that proper timing is a necessity for profitable trading. In over 35 years of active trading, I have yet to see any approach that has consistently beaten our technique's awesome accuracy in timing the market's turns. Combining the perspective given by an accurate Elliott wave count with an understanding of what is actually happening in the market (the Profitunity windows) and with our own fractal analysis, a trader can be "on top" of the market minute by minute (or day by day, if that is the preferred time frame).

It is the best of both worlds when you work the market from both sides—profit buildup and risk reduction. The Profitunity approach to wave analysis provides a quantitative and qualitative measurement of the risk involved in any specific trade. Knowing where you are in the Elliott wave real time (not after the fact) gives you the knowledge to cut through rumors, opinions, announcements, and myths to get at the basics of how the market is unfolding. Some traders, even with this knowledge, lack training in the emotional–logical balance required for successful trading. To most traders, emotional management is the most difficult barrier to profitable trading. This barrier will be specifically addressed in Chapters 10 and 11, when we examine the proficient and expert levels of trading.

Our purpose in this chapter is to build a framework that shows why the market does what it does. Learning to ride the market waves is similar to surfing. The bigger the wave you ride, the more chance you'll have a "wipeout." An occasional water dunk is the price you pay to master this sport. All surfers know that the more often they go out to sea to meet the "monsters," the more they will learn how to read the behavior of each wave. The more you understand how to use and how to dissipate the energy contained in each trading "monster," the more confidence you'll have in any unexpected situation.

THE ELLIOTT WAVE

The primary reason to be interested in understanding the Elliott wave is that it is the best indicator of where you are in the market's movement from down to up and back down again. Reading the market is like trying to understand how New York City functions. You could spend one day with each of the five borough presidents, to get an in-depth understanding of what is happening in each borough at that time. Another approach would be to take a helicopter and view the entire city from about the height of the World Trade Center. The Profitunity approach is comparable to in-depth interviews: we find out what is happening in the "lives" of individual commodities at the present time. The Elliott wave takes us to a higher altitude and shows, from a wider viewpoint, how the market is operating.

The Elliott wave has received considerable discussion through the years. Many derogatory comments have come from those who don't profit from using it because they don't understand what it is and how it works. The Elliott wave is an analysis of the underlying structure of the market. As we will see in Chapter 8, the Elliott wave is the underlying structure of the market, and the fractal is the underlying structure of the Elliott wave.

R. N. Elliott, for whom this approach is named, studied the markets for years, searching for some repeatable pattern that would let him pick the tops and bottoms. The Elliott wave is a top and bottom picker. Normally, this is dangerous to your financial health, as most Elliott students will document.

A. J. Frost and Robert Prechtor (1978) described the Elliott wave and the personalities of the various waves. They gave excellent documentation and description of the Elliott wave, but did not give specific directions as to *how to trade* the Elliott wave profitably. When their work was published, I read it at least a dozen times. At that time, I was developing the MFI and I decided to do some research on the differences between the waves as measured by the MFI.

Basic Rhythms of the Elliott Wave

The Elliott sequence consists of a basic rhythm of "fives" corrected by "threes." This sequence remains constant no matter what degree of wave is being analyzed. This wave rhythm is observable as long as there is a minimum amount of trading volume. As a rule of thumb, we use a minimum average of 20 ticks per time period, although the Elliott sequence can often be seen in a shorter period market with much less volume—for example, the one-minute chart.

Even more important than the time scale is the "form" of the patterns. Waves can be stretched or compressed (both in time and price), but the underlying form remains constant. A movement will unfold in its primary direction in a series of 5 waves, labeled 1 through 5. A 5-wave movement is normally corrected by a 3-wave movement in the opposite direction. The numbered waves (1–5) were called "cardinal waves" by Elliott. Frost and Prechtor popularized the term "impulse waves" for waves 1, 3, and 5. Corrective waves are designated with small letters (a, b, c, d, e).

As shown in Figure 7–1, the first wave is corrected by wave 2, and wave 3 is corrected by wave 4. Then the 5-wave sequence is corrected by a 3-wave sequence, labeled a-b-c.

After a 5-wave sequence is complete, it will usually become a wave of "larger degree," or a wave contributing to a larger wave. The complete movement of waves 1 through 5 will complete the next higher tier of wave sequences. Therefore, the movement from wave 1 to wave 5 completes a wave 1, a wave 3, or a wave 5, and the a-b-c sequence completes either a wave 2 or a wave 4. (See Figure 7–2.)

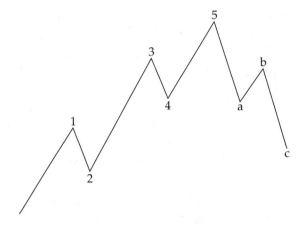

Figure 7–1 Diagram of waves 1–5 with an a-b-c correction.

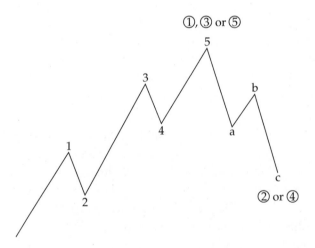

Figure 7–2 A 5-wave sequence with a 3-wave correction can be part of another wave of larger degree.

Characteristics of the Different Waves

The basic rules of wave theory are simple enough, but the applications of these rules daunt most wave theory students. By using the Profitunity indicators explained in the previous chapter, this job becomes simple, concise, and accurate. One of the greatest pleasures in trading is to watch your wave count unfold just the way you anticipated. Many of the relationships that most Elliotticians discuss are really tendencies, and they are neither permanent nor precise. In addition, these relationships change over time. Just as you begin to count on them and place money on your interpretation, they change. We have solved this problem.

Before we explain our solution, let's examine the various waves and the relationships among those waves. Again, I must emphasize that some of the concepts that make our Elliott wave analysis much more accurate is our reliance on the Profitunity indicators that describe market participation in the present tense.

Wave 1

First waves are always a change-in-trend movement. The first traders who get into the new trend are always running the "Have Fun" psychological program explained in Chapter 12. The beginning of wave 1 (which is either the end of a wave 5 or the end of a wave c or e, coming from the opposite direction) will be accompanied by a divergence in our MFI oscillator. Once we have all the indicators in place, we expect a sharp move off the bottom (top). This may also be a *point zero* (see the Profitunity Planned Trading (PPT) technique in Level Three, Chapter 9), which allows us even more trading and profit opportunities.

The best way to anticipate and target the end of a wave 1 is to examine the internal structure and waves of a smaller degree. Look at a smaller time frame; for example, look for the 5-wave sequence inside of the developing wave 1 (Figure 7–3). Then check out (1) the divergence, (2) the target zone, (3) the fractals, (4) the squats, and (5) a change in the momentum indicator. We call these our *five magic bullets* because they almost always kill the current trend.

Wave 2

Once the first wave has finished, we anticipate a second wave in the opposite direction. Second waves are created by new selling (buying)—as opposed to fourth waves, which are created by profit taking (long liquidation or short covering). Wave 2 targets can be generated by (1) Fibonacci relationship and (2) internal wave counts.

The most common targets for the end of wave 2 are between 38 percent and 62 percent retracement of the range of wave 1 (Figure 7–4). About three out of four wave 2s will end in this

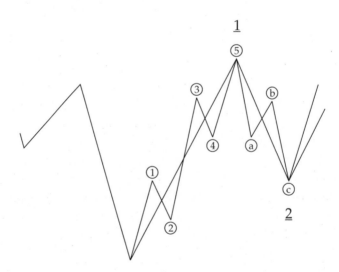

Figure 7–3 Characteristics of wave 1.

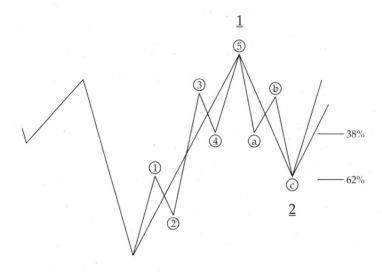

Figure 7–4 The most common retracement of wave 2.

area; only about one in six will retrace more than 62 percent. Another tip is that if wave 2 ends with less than a 38 percent correction, wave 2 will usually be an irregular correction (see Figure 7–11, later in this chapter).

Again, wave 2 is produced by new selling in an up trend (or buying in a down trend) by traders who are not in the market and do not recognize that this up move is a wave 1 in a new direction (see the section on finding point zero, in Chapter 9). These traders believe wave 1 is simply another correction in a continuing down move, so they sell at the top of wave 1. This is why wave 2 behaves quite differently from wave 4, which is a profit-taking wave. Traders in the market with profits will take more time getting out than traders seeing new opportunities in the market. It is extremely important to target accurately the end of wave 2: the greatest profit-taking opportunities per unit of time happen in wave 3, which generally moves faster and travels a greater distance.

Wave 3

Robert Prechtor calls wave 3 ". . . a wonder to behold." Wave 3 gives us great profit opportunities. When we reach Level Five (Chapter 12), we will analyze the psychological properties that accompany wave 3.

One way to recognize a wave 3 is by its slope. It is generally steeper (going through price changes faster) than a wave 1. Wave 3s sometimes seem almost vertical (Figure 7–5), and can be mistaken for wave 5 blow-offs (sell-offs). Generally, a wave 3 has heavy volume. If a powerful, fast move is accompanied by less volume, it usually is a blow-off (sell-off). During wave 3, the economic background begins to support the move (this is not true during wave 1). Fundamental reasons begin to pile atop the technical indicators. These are the most immensely profitable times to be in the market and it is imperative to "load the wagon" on these waves.

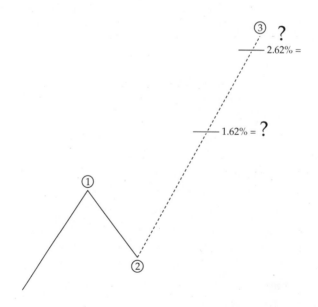

Figure 7–5 Characteristics of wave 3.

The best initial targets for the length of wave 3 are between 1 and 1.62 times the length of wave 1. Rarely will wave 3 be shorter than wave 1, and often it will be longer than 1.62 times the length of wave 1. The best way to target the end of wave 3 is to go to a smaller time frame and use a confluence of the five magic bullets to find the end of the fifth wave of wave 3 indicators. These magic bullets are:

1. Divergence in our MFI oscillator;

2. Location inside the target zone;

3. Formation of a fractal on the top (bottom);

4. A squat in one of the three topmost (lowest) bars;

5. A change in direction of the momentum on the Profitunity moving average convergence divergence (MACD).

Wave 4

Once the powerful wave 3 is over, profit taking enters the picture. The most skillful traders were into the trend earliest, and therefore are sitting on ample profits. The character of wave 4 is entirely different from that of wave 2. Elliott labeled this difference as the rule of alternation: If wave 2 is simple, wave 4 will be complex, and vice versa. A simple correction is usually considered to be a zigzag. If that happens in wave 2, wave 4 should be a complex sideways correction (flat, irregular, triangle, double or triple threes).

In our research, we found that 85 percent of all whiplashes occur during wave 4. If you simply cannot come up with any idea where you are in the wave count, you most likely are in a wave 4. If you wake up and are in a wave 4, the best strategy might be to go back to bed. However, as this is being written, several commodities have been in wave 4s on the monthly charts for years. I am not willing to stay in bed that long.

Besides, if we can target the end of a wave 4, we will have great profit opportunities to trade wave 5.

The retracement percentages on wave 4 (Figure 7–6) are quite different from those on wave 2. Generally, wave 4 corrections last much longer—often, up to 70 percent as long (timewise) as the entire 5-wave sequence you are watching. Wave 4s generally do not retrace as much, pricewise, as wave 2. Again, this is caused by profit taking rather than new entries into the market. You generally see a precipitous drop in volume, volatility, option premiums, and momentum indicators.

Only about one in six wave 4s retraces less than 38 percent of wave 3. The most likely target is between 38 percent and 50 percent. In watching wave 4 develop, remember that an "unbreakable" rule is that wave 4 never goes below the top of wave 1. In actual trading, you will see a number of instances where the rule does not hold true.

In analyzing wave 4 to get good trade location to trade wave 5, use the Fibonacci relationships and look for the five magic bullets on a smaller time frame inside wave c of wave 4. Make sure that you have between 100 and 140 bars in the c wave. You get that number by manipulating the time frame on the chart.

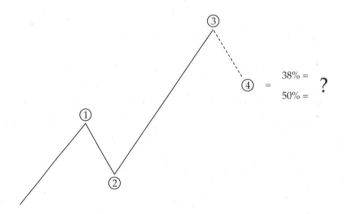

Figure 7–6   Wave 4 retracements.

Once more, the five magic bullets are:

1. MFI divergence;

2. Location inside the target zone;

3. Fractal;

4. Squat;

5. Change in momentum on the Profitunity MACD.

Wave 5

Wave 5, shown in Figure 7–7, is the traders' last struggle to create new high (low) prices. It is not as enthusiastic or euphoric as wave 3. Generally, the slope of the price line is less steep than in wave 3. Professional traders are using these new price thrusts to take their profits while the nonprofessionals are still getting into the trend. The end of wave 5 is calculated by a variety of methods already mentioned. When these different

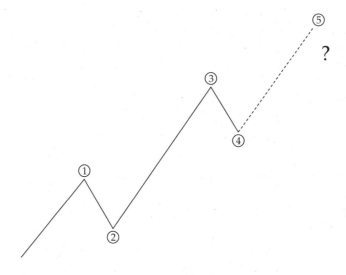

Figure 7–7   Characteristics of wave 5.

113

methods form targets that are in a tight cluster, confidence goes up that we can forecast the terminal point of wave 5. The length of wave 5 is measured from the bottom of wave 4, so no final targets can be projected until wave 4 has ended. (The next section, on combining the MFI oscillator with the Elliott wave, gives the minimum requirements for wave 4.)

One of the most accurate predictors of the end of wave 5 is the *target zone.* I learned of this methodology from Tom Joseph of Trading Techniques, Inc. (677 W. Turkeyfoot Lake Road, Akron, Ohio 44319), and have found it to be extremely useful and profitable. Measure the difference in price between the start of wave 1 and the end of wave 3 (waves 0–3). Then add this measurement to the bottom of wave 4. Take 62 percent of the length of that difference, and add it to the bottom of wave 4 also. The vast majority of times, wave 5 will end between those two numbers. You can even improve on this accuracy by doing the same procedure inside of the fifth wave of wave 5. This will give you an even smaller target zone. Normally, the smaller zone from the five waves inside the larger wave 5 will fall inside the larger target zone from the larger degree waves. This narrows your target zone even more. Next, by adding the Profitunity indicators of the fractal and squat, plus the divergence between wave 3 and wave 5, you can get very precise profit-taking and trade-entry points.

The complete movement of waves 1 through 5 will usually complete the next higher tier of wave sequences. Therefore, the movement from wave 1 to wave 5 completes a wave 1, a wave 3, or a wave 5, and the a-b-c sequence completes either a wave 2 or a wave 4 (see Figure 7–8).

Corrections

Corrections are normally classified as simple or complex. Simple refers to zigzag corrections, and complex refers to everything else. In a-b-c three-wave corrections, whether simple or

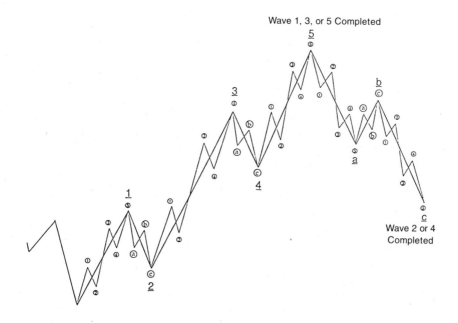

Figure 7–8   Impulse and corrective waves of various degrees.

complex, the b wave always contains three waves, and the c wave always contains five waves. The a wave may contain either three waves or five waves. If it contains five waves, that is your tipoff that it is going to be a zigzag type correction. If it contains three waves, it most likely will be a flat, irregular, or triangle correction.

Simple (Zigzag) Corrections

Once the five waves of wave a are finished, the b wave correction normally will not retrace more than 62 percent of the length of wave a (Figure 7–9). In rare instances, it may correct to 75 percent. Because wave c shares the characteristics of wave 3, it can be a profitable trading format. If wave b ends between 50 percent and 62 percent of wave a, look for a fractal and a

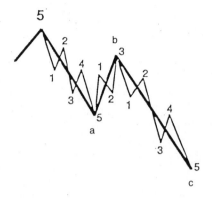

Wave a of a zigzag pattern is always five waves.

Therefore, if five waves can be identified in wave a, expect a tradable zigzag pattern to materialize.

Figure 7–9   Simple (zigzag) correction.

squat to establish an entry for trading wave c. Then trade wave c just as you would any other five-wave sequence.

Use the five magic bullets to take profit at the end of wave c of wave 4, and reverse to trade wave 5 in the opposite direction.

Complex Corrections

There are three types of complex corrections: (1) flat correction (Figure 7–10), (2) irregular correction (Figure 7–11), and (3) triangle correction (Figures 7–12 and 7–13).

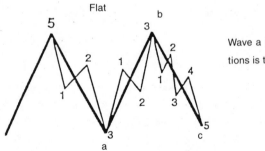

Wave a in other types of corrections is three waves.

Figure 7–10   Flat correction.

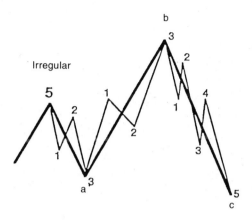

Figure 7–11   Irregular correction.

In a flat correction, each wave is almost identical/equal. If wave b exceeds the high of the last impulse wave, you can suspect an irregular correction.

Triangle corrections are five-wave patterns labeled a-b-c-d-e. They usually occur in the next to the last wave sequence—wave 4 or wave b. When triangles occur in wave 4, prices tend to shoot out in the direction of the impulse wave 3 being corrected (Figure 7–12). When triangles occur in wave b, prices tend to shoot out in the direction of the correction wave a being corrected (Figure 7–13).

We have examined the characteristics and typical formations of both the impulse and the corrective waves. Next, we need to find easy and profitable techniques of entering trades to maximize the predictability given by accurate analysis of wave structure.

TAKING THE AMBIGUITY OUT OF THE ELLIOTT WAVE

I have had great personal interest in the Elliott wave since the first time I saw some old photocopies of R. N. Elliott's market

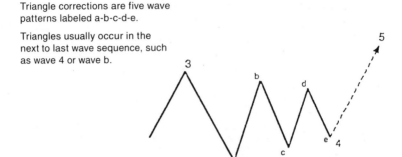

Triangle corrections are five wave patterns labeled a-b-c-d-e.

Triangles usually occur in the next to last wave sequence, such as wave 4 or wave b.

When triangles occur in wave 4, prices tend to shoot out in the direction of the impulse wave 3 being corrected.

Figure 7–12   Wave 4 triangle correction.

comments, long before Frost and Prechtor wrote their book. The Elliott wave made sense but was of little use in trading the market. I attributed my inability to count waves accurately to my lack of knowledge and/or experience.

Several things bothered me about the Elliott wave. First, Elliotticians don't actually count the waves themselves; they count the price change that a wave covers. In the example

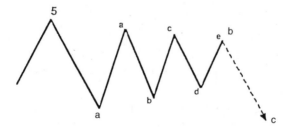

When triangles occur in wave b, prices tend to shoot out in the direction of the correction wave a being corrected.

Figure 7–13   Wave b triangle.

118

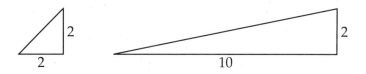

Figure 7–14 Two units high vs. two units wide (left), and two units high vs. ten units wide (right).

shown in Figure 7–14, a wave that is two units high and two units wide (the time dimension) would be counted the same as a wave two units high and ten units wide. One thing is certain: while they both would be counted as two units high, they are not the same type of market.

The height of a wave is always counted on the vertical axis, ignoring the time factor. When the time factor is counted, each wave produces a right triangle (Figure 7–15). In studying this, I noticed that there seemed to be a relationship between the area created by the price and the time change of each wave.

This studying was going on in the early 1980s, and I was using a handheld calculator to work out the areas. I found that if you take the area under wave 1 and add it to the area of wave

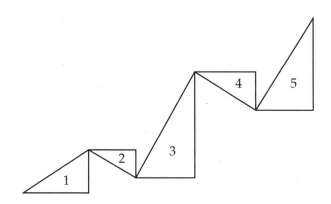

Figure 7–15 Areas beneath the Elliott Waves.

2, your answer will tend to equal or have a Fibonacci relationship (usually 62 percent) to the area of wave 3. Then, by subtracting the area of wave 4 from the area of wave 3, you end up
with the area wave or a Fibonacci relationship.

Armed with this insight, I hired a computer programmer to
write the software to calculate and predict the end of the following wave. When we input the beginning and ending prices
of wave 1 and counted the number of bars on the time frame I
was trading (usually 60-minute bars), the computer would calculate three different time–price targets for the end of wave 2.
It also would automatically rank-order these projections, based
on probability.

This one step put me quantum leaps ahead in trading the
Elliott wave.

COMBINING THE MFI WITH
THE ELLIOTT WAVE

As noted earlier, one of the key indicators we use in Profitunity trading is the Market Facilitation Index (MFI). This is a
basic measure of how effectively the current trading volume is
moving price through time. It is an indicator of tick (gas)
mileage. The higher the MFI, the more the price changes for
each unit of volume. We want our money invested in the market when the price is moving the fastest, giving us the maximum rate of return. The MFI (explained in Chapter 6) is the
range divided by the volume, and the answer is compared to
the previous time period. After working with this indicator for
several years, we noticed that there was a different range in
each of the Elliott waves.

Most traders, even professional Elliotticians, sometimes
find counting the waves on a price chart quite frustrating. I
sought a better, more convenient, more accurate, and less subjective measure to count the waves. My next idea was to calculate the MFI in each wave, by averaging the MFI bars and then

comparing the different averages for the different waves. I found exactly what I had anticipated.

The average MFI was highest during wave 3. On wave 1 and wave 5, this average was less. It was clear that there was a divergence between the price at the end of wave 5 and the average MFI for wave 5. Although the price was higher at the end of wave 5 than at the end of wave 3, the average MFI for wave 5 was less, creating a divergence (Figure 7–16). This divergence became an advance indicator for the end of this impulse series and forecasted a change in trend. Having identified a set of parameters, we were then able to trade from them or build an indicator to identify this difference between the market facilitation in each wave. This has been done successfully with the MFI. The MFI is a true present-tense momentum indicator.

Most of the "off-the-shelf" indicators, such as stochastics, RSI, and so on, do not compare momentum. They compare the current price with the price *x* bars ago. *They do not compare the*

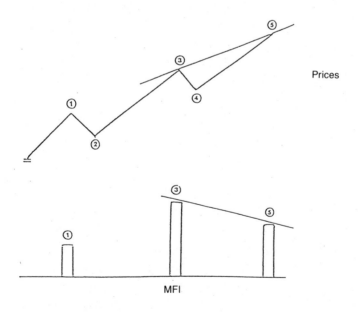

Figure 7–16 Average MFI divergence between wave 3 and wave 5.

rate of internal price action inside wave 5 to that inside wave 3. Therefore, the more traditional indicators used by traders today *will not* consistently show the end of a trend, the most crucial information in trading.

Tom Joseph, an excellent researcher in trading techniques, has generated a very effective momentum indicator. He takes a 35-bar moving average and subtracts it from a 5-bar moving average. This produces an oscillator that is programmable on most quote machines. The 5-period average smoothes and represents the current strength of the market, and the 35-bar moving average indicates the momentum strength over a longer period. We have found that if we change the numbers to a 5-bar/34-bar (5/34) oscillator, we get an extremely close approximation of the difference found by the more laborious job of averaging the MFI for each wave.

For example, assume that you are currently in a wave 3. The 5-period moving average represents the rate of movement inside the wave 3. This rate of change, like the MFI, is moving faster than at any other time in the Elliott wave sequence. The 34-period moving average represents the rate movement or MFI inside waves 1 and 2. This rate of change is much slower than the 5-period rate, creating a large difference between the two moving averages. Wave 3 produces the highest peak in the 5/34 oscillator. Over the years, we have tinkered with this oscillator in a number of ways.

The 5/34/5 Profitunity MACD

We found that, by adding a 5-period moving average to the oscillator, we changed the oscillator into a moving average convergence divergence (MACD). This last average becomes a "signal line" or an indicator of market rhythm (discussed in Chapter 9), which allows us further confidence in the trades we are placing. It gives a *leading indicator*, showing exactly where the market begins to run out of steam. This signal will happen

122

before there is a directional (momentum) change observable in the price. The 5/34/5 Profitunity MACD tells instantly which side of the market we should be on.

There are four primary uses for the 5/34/5 Profitunity MACD:

1. Identifying the peak of wave 3;

2. Determining the end of wave 4, or when its minimum requirements have been met;

3. Looking for the end of a trend and the top of wave 5;

4. Signaling immediately the direction of the current momentum, or which side of the market the trader wishes to trade.

Identifying the Peak of Wave 3

In a five-wave sequence, both the average MFI and the 5/34/5 Profitunity MACD will peak at the top of wave 3 (see Figure 7–17). If we place the 5/34 oscillator in a histogram format, we can easily determine the bar on which the peak occurs. Because all oscillators are lagging indicators, the peak of wave 3 will be the highest (lowest) price that occurs between 1 and 5 bars prior to the peak in the oscillator.

Immediately after the peak, we notice the histogram moving below the signal line. The signal line is the 5-bar average of the oscillator itself. When this happens, be careful about placing any longs: the momentum is running out of steam. If long, you may choose to hold on through wave 4 or you may decide to take your profits and wait until this oscillator indicates that the minimum requirements for wave 4 have been met.

Determining the End of Wave 4

After the end of wave 3, the oscillator will pull back with the retracing wave 4. The histogram will fall below the signal line,

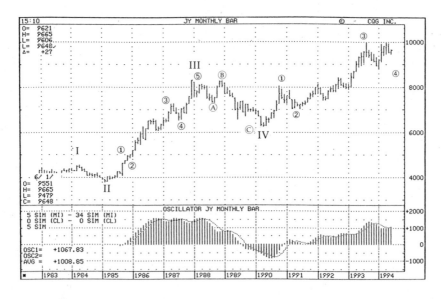

Figure 7–17 The 5/34/5 profitunity MACD peaking on wave 3.

telling us that this is not a good place to initiate a long position. However, we must address one more important consideration here. The 5/34/5 Profitunity MACD is a very accurate indicator for the Elliott wave, providing the user understands how this indicator works. *It is always measuring an Elliott wave.* The question arises: *Which degree of Elliott wave?* Our research indicates that, for the most accurate measurement, the wave under consideration should occupy from 100 to 140 bars. If we are looking at a wave sequence of fewer than 100 bars, the MACD will be measuring the Elliott wave of a larger degree. If the wave sequence occupies more than 140 bars, the MACD will be measuring an Elliott wave of a smaller degree.

As an example, Figure 7–18 is an hourly chart of the Japanese yen. In examining the move from point X to point Y, we are looking for the next profitable trade. Assume that you are not in this market at the moment. It appears to be a five-wave move-up covering the last six trading days.

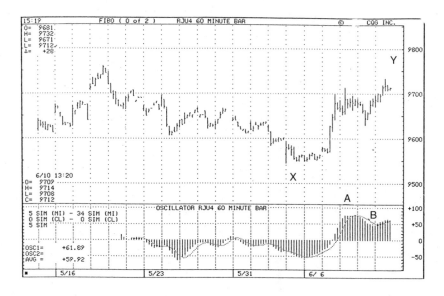

Figure 7–18   Japanese yen, hourly chart.

The first question might be: Are you sure that wave 4 is over? The 5/34/5 Profitunity MACD will give you a definite answer only if you have the appropriate number of bars (100–140) on the screen. From point X to point Y, there are only 33 bars. Notice, though, that the MACD peaks at point A but does not cross the zero line at point B. Because we have only 33 bars on the hourly chart and we need at least four times that many, we can tab down to a 15-minute chart (Figure 7–19) to get a precise reading.

Figure 7–19 shows the same Japanese yen on a 15-minute chart containing 102 bars between points X and Y. There are two important activities to notice in this chart. First, the MACD has crossed the zero line at point R, telling us that the minimum requirements for wave 4 have been met. Thus, early in the trading day on June 9, we could start looking for a good trade location to go long.

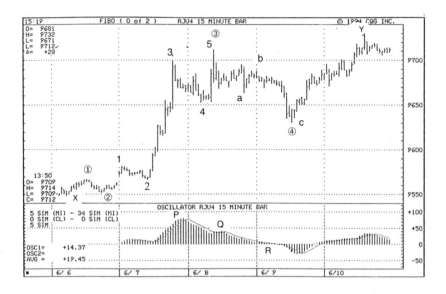

Figure 7–19 Japanese yen, 15-minute chart.

Second, this chart gives vital information about what is happening between points P and Q. There is divergence (the price is higher but the oscillator is not), but the oscillator does not go back to zero. This occurrence indicates that point P is wave 3 of wave 3, and wave 5 of wave 3 is at point Q. This knowledge will save you from the most common mistakes Elliotticians make: counting wave 3 inside of wave 3 as the end of the third wave, and then counting wave 5 of wave 3 as a larger degree wave 5.

When that happens, the Elliotticians are short at point ④. The market finishes wave 4 and they get "creamed" because of that error in their count.

Assuming that you found a good trade location based on the crossover of the zero line and you have the appropriate number of bars in the wave count, you are ready to start planning your profit taking. To count more precisely the waves between points ④ and ⑤, we must consult a 5-minute chart and get enough bars to count wave 5 of wave 5. From Figure 7–20,

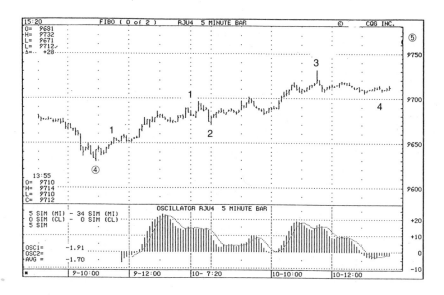

Figure 7–20 Japanese yen, 5-minute chart.

we can see that we are in the fourth wave of wave ⑤. We have fulfilled the minimum requirements for wave 4 of wave ⑤ (again, as noted by the MACD crossing the zero line), and we can estimate the target zone for the end of wave 5 of wave ⑤.

These three charts (Figures 7–18 through 7–20) deserve careful study. If you have a thorough understanding of this approach, you will maximize your profits and minimize the risk you need to take. Your entries and exits will generate the confidence needed to move to higher levels of trading.

Remember, once you have your wave sequence in the proper perspective (100–140 bars for the wave series you are counting), you can determine when the minimum requirements for wave 4 have been met, that is, when the oscillator crosses the zero line. An important note here: the oscillator crosses the zero line after a peak in wave 3 indicates the *minimum requirements* for wave 4 have been met. It *does not* indicate that wave 4 is over, and it would be premature to place a trade for wave 5 until after this indicator has crossed the zero line.

To increase the preciseness of entering a trade at the end of wave 4, look for the a-b-c or triangle correction. Further, look inside the last wave (c; or e, if in a triangle) for the five magic bullets inside of that smaller wave.

Another way to anticipate the end of wave 4 is to look at the Fibonacci time projections. First, measure (timewise) the distance between the peaks of wave 1 and wave 3. Then multiply this distance by two Fibonacci ratios. You will find that most wave 4s will end in the time period between 1.38 and 1.62 times the length from the peak of wave 1 to the peak of wave 3 when measured from the bottom of wave 2. Putting all these indicators together will give you an excellent target zone, both

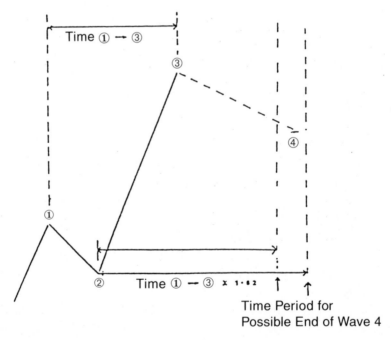

Figure 7–21   A timing model for estimating the end of wave 4.

in time and price, for the ending of wave 4 (Figure 7–21). You then can put on low-risk trade for taking advantage of wave 5.

Looking for the End of a Trend and the Top of Wave 5

After wave 4 is over and wave 5 gets under way, we can begin estimating targets for the end of this five-wave sequence. First, measure the price distance from the *beginning* of wave 1 to the *end* of wave 3. Take this number and add it to the end of wave 4. Then, mark off 62 percent of this distance. Between these two numbers (62 percent and 100 percent of the price distance from the beginning of wave 1 to the end of wave 3, added to the beginning of wave 4) is the best target for the end of wave 5.

Next, count the five waves inside wave 5. Repeat the above measurements for each of the five waves inside wave 5. This will give you a smaller target zone for the completion of both wave 5 and wave 5 of wave 5 (Figure 7–22). Remember that all trends end in a divergence between price high and oscillator high at the end of wave 5.

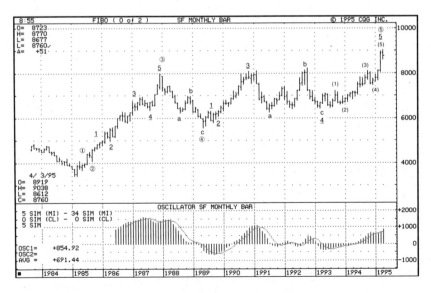

Figure 7–22   The end of wave (5) of wave 5 of wave ⑤.

Signaling Immediately the Direction of the Current Momentum

Here, we must first determine the relative position between the 5/34 histogram of the oscillator and the signal line (the signal line is the 5-bar simple moving average of the 5/34 oscillator) and then take trades only in the direction of the current momentum. (See Figure 7–23.) This technique is the most sensitive and accurate filter for measures of change in momentum. If the histogram is below the signal line, we only take shorts. If the histogram is above the signal line, we only take longs.

We need to look at one more small detail to increase our accuracy in counting the waves. When the proportion of bars (100–140) is correct and we see a divergence that does not go back to the zero line, what we are seeing is a wave 3 peak inside a larger wave 3. The MACD will retrace (but not to zero), then come back and generate a divergence, telling us that it is wave 5 of wave 3 and therefore the peak of larger wave 3 is at that

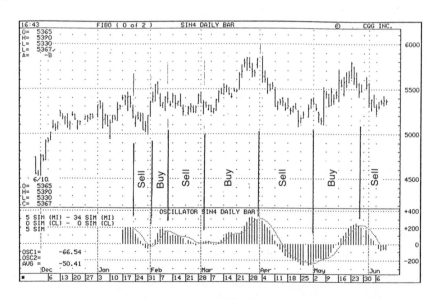

Figure 7–23 Determining the immediate market momentum.

point. Again, the most common mistake Elliotticians make is confusing the peak of wave 5 inside a larger wave 3 for the end of wave 5. Based on this error, they take new positions in the opposite direction and are killed as the real wave 5 evolves and stops them out.

After finishing wave 5 inside the larger wave 3, the MACD will come back to zero line for the indication that the minimum requirements for the larger wave 4 have been met. Wave 4 will often end near the end of the wave 4 inside the larger wave 3. If this point is near a common Fibonacci retracement, it gives more credibility to this target.

With skill in trading this MACD, you can throw away your stochastics, RSI, momentum indicators, and similar tools. Nothing comes close to the accuracy demonstrated by this MACD. This indicator alone should be invaluable to any serious trader.

This divergence pattern happens many times every day in every commodity. It is priceless for both intraday and longer-term position trading.

In Chapter 10, we will put together in a single format (the Profitunity Trading Partner) everything we have discussed thus far and add two more indicators.

SUMMARY

In this chapter, we examined the Elliott wave by looking at the basic rhythms the market follows. Next, we analyzed the characteristics of the individual waves and introduced a tool that takes the ambiguity out of wave counting.

We focused on the four uses of the 5/34/5 Profitunity MACD and reviewed charts that illustrated its capabilities.

In the next chapter, we will examine the underlying structure of the Elliott wave, which is the fractal. We will learn how to trade the Elliott wave even if we don't know exactly where we are in the wave count.

REVIEW QUESTIONS

1. What are the three "unbreakable" rules of Elliott wave analysis? Which one is often broken?

2. Which one of the three corrective wave patterns should always contain three waves? Which should always contain five waves? Which may contain either five or three waves? If that wave has five waves, what can you conclude about the type of correction needed?

3. What are the most common (therefore most expected) Fibonacci ratios in wave b of (a) zigzag, (b) flat, and (c) irregular correction?

4. What are the most common (therefore most expected) Fibonacci ratios in wave c of (a) zigzag, (b) flat, and (c) irregular correction?

5. What is the best way to trade a triangle correction?

6. Describe the characteristics of wave 1, wave 2, wave 3, wave 4, and wave 5.

7. What oscillator most closely matches and gives you an on-line instant readout of the average MFI?

8. What advantage does an MFI have over an oscillator?

9. What vital information does the signal line on the 5/34/5 Profitunity MACD give?

10. What four important bits of trading information does the 5/34/5 Profitunity MACD offer both long-term and short-term traders?

11. On what number of divergences will most trends end?

8

Using Fractals and Leverage

"Come to the edge of the cliff," he said.
"We're afraid," they said.
"Come to the edge of the cliff," he said.
"We're afraid," they said.
"Come to the edge of the cliff," he said.
They came.
He pushed.
They flew.

Guillaume Appolinaire

GOALS:

1. **TO UNDERSTAND AND BE ABLE TO RECOGNIZE AND TRADE THE INITIATING AND RESPONSIVE FRACTAL PATTERNS;**

2. **TO UNDERSTAND HOW LEVERAGE EITHER SIGNALS A TRADE OR CANCELS A POTENTIAL TRADE.**

Commodity traders and system sellers have a knack for taking any new development and applying it to trading. Most of the time, these developments do not prove to be profitable and become just another passing fad. In the past, markets have gone through various forms of technical indicators that have either died or lapsed into nonuse because they were not profitable.

The early 1980s produced the $3,000 black box systems, RSI, stochastics, sentiment indexes, and so on. Then Trade Station and other program developers made back testing and curve fitting a fun project for new traders. Mechanical systems were the rage—popular but not profitable. Along came Market Profile, which snared thousands of otherwise intelligent traders into losing money. They lost because Market Profile uses parametric statistics based on the assumption that the market is random. Parametric statistics are not appropriate to examine nonlinear behavior. Astrology keeps raising its head when new computer programs are sold and then dying back from nonuse. Finding that nothing new seems to work, many traders become attracted to something very old called Candlesticks. Unfortunately, the average trader does not make profits using it.

Chaos and fractals offer a very different outlook. All other approaches are based on traditional Aristotelian philosophy. Chaos and the markets are both "natural" phenomena. Once you thoroughly understand the markets and how they work, you will understand why all the linear systems either don't work from the beginning or die an early death.

For the past dozen or so years, the Profitunity Trading Group has been conducting intensive research into the theory of chaos and quantum mechanics as applied to trading the markets. With the aid of two PhDs in theoretical math and computer science, and using a mainframe computer, we were able to pinpoint the underlying structure (fractal) of the Elliott wave. We used sophisticated nonlinear feedback calculus programs to extract the exact fractal points in the chart. Next, we sifted through thousands of charts on which the fractals had been located via computer, to see whether there were any consistent pattern formations at the fractals.

We found a pattern that accurately reflects over 98 percent of the fractals found by the computer. This pattern recognition allows one to trade the fractals without a mainframe computer. We are presently one of very few groups to apply this theory to real-time trading in various markets. Sparing you the theories, concepts, and experiments that led to our discovery of the fractal of the Elliott wave, let's move on to what a fractal looks like and how to trade it.

Market or "behavioral" fractals indicate a significant behavior change. When you decide to exit a losing trade, where you will get out is quite predictable. You will exit a losing trade when the pain of losing one more dollar is more intense than the pain of saying you were wrong in taking the trade. That point is a behavioral fractal. A fractal also occurs when you pick up the phone to tell your broker to place an order. A behavioral fractal occurred whenever you decided to read this book rather than choosing some other activity. A decision to trade is always a behavioral fractal. To trade profitably, we need to recognize the behavioral fractal of masses of traders and understand the impending change in the bias of the market. We can then place orders before or during the early beginnings of a new trend move. We can examine our individual "psychological" fractals on a personal basis, and we can analyze the market's "sociological" fractals from evidence on a bar chart.

THE INITIATING FRACTAL PATTERN

A fractal pattern on a bar chart (of any time span) consists of a minimum of five consecutive bars. Our working definition of this initiating fractal is that the middle bar must have a higher high (or lower low) than the two preceding bars and the two following bars. It may look like any of the examples in Figure 8–1. It is important to note the following restrictions:

1. If a bar's high is parallel to the middle or high (low) bar, it does not count as one of the five bars in the fractal

because it does not have a lower high (higher low) than the middle bar;

2. Two adjacent fractals may share bars.

In Figure 8–1, notice that pattern A shows a pristine fractal where the two preceding and the two following bars have lower highs than the middle bar. This sets up an up fractal, designated by (∧). Pattern B is also an up fractal, but the same formation also creates a down fractal (∨). This happens because the two preceding bars and the two following bars are "inside" bars. They fulfill the requirement that the middle bar must be

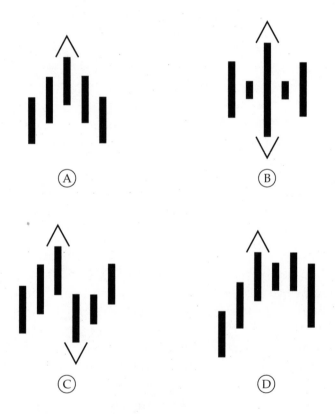

Figure 8–1   Examples of initiating fractals.

the highest or lowest of the minimum five-bar sequence. Pattern C shows another formation that creates both an up fractal and a down fractal. As shown, these fractals may "share" bars. Pattern D requires six bars to form an up fractal because the fifth bar has a high equal to the previous high. Remember the working definition:

> A fractal must have two preceding and two following bars with lower highs (higher lows, on a down move).

In an up fractal, we are interested only in the bar's high. In a down fractal, we are interested only in the bar's low.

When the market is making a bullish upward move, puts in a top, and then starts back down with two bars that have lower highs, that market has made a fractal decision. (See Figure 8–2.) It has gone up to point A and, for whatever reasons, has

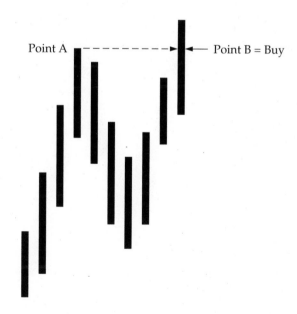

Figure 8–2   Fractal buy signal.

turned back down. Should the market again move up and then go beyond (higher) the price at point A, the pattern indicates that the market has changed its mind and decided to recant its earlier decision to stop at point A. One tick above point A then becomes a breakout buy.

Any five-bar sequence in which the middle bar is higher (or lower) than the two preceding and two following bars forms a fractal, and once a fractal is formed it will remain a fractal. During the lifetime of this fractal, it may play several roles. It can, from time to time, be a *fractal start*, a *fractal signal*, or a *fractal stop*. The role it currently is playing depends on where it is located in the sequence of the market's up-and-down movement.

Definitions

Before going further, we must define these various roles that a fractal can play:

Fractal start is any fractal that is followed by a fractal in the opposite direction (see Figure 8–3).

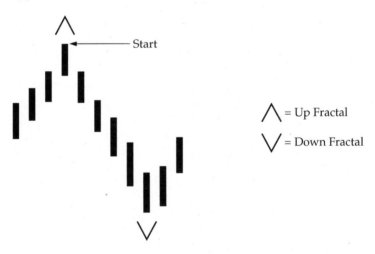

Figure 8–3   Fractal start.

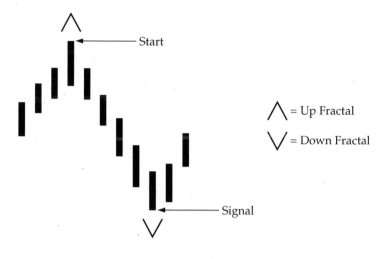

Figure 8–4 Fractal signal.

Fractal signal is any fractal that follows a fractal in the opposite direction (see Figure 8–4).

Whenever an up fractal, for example, is followed by a down fractal, what happens in between is always an Elliott wave of one degree or another. Notice that a fractal start and a fractal signal are always generated at the same time.

Fractal stop is the most distant fractal peak of the last two fractals in the opposite direction. Usually, but not always, this will be two fractals back in the opposite direction. Figure 8–5 shows both cases.

LEVERAGE

Now we are ready to examine the concept of "leverage." First, think of a number-one wood, the golf club you use for maximum distance. What makes it possible to drive the golf ball hundreds of yards down the fairway? A combination of strength, coordination, and the leverage of the golf club (Figure

Figure 8–5   Fractal stop.

8–6). Pretend for a moment that you are in a crazy golf tournament. The rules are different here: every time you drive the ball, the caddy saws 6 inches off the handle of your driver. After a few holes, your score will go up because you are giving up leverage every time you make a drive.

Let's apply the same principle to the market. Whenever you have a fractal start and a fractal signal, you have leverage (see Figure 8–7). If the market comes back toward the fractal start, you lose a bit of leverage. If the market comes all the way back to the topmost (bottommost) bar of the start *plus one tick,* you have lost all your leverage and the buy or sell signal is immediately canceled.

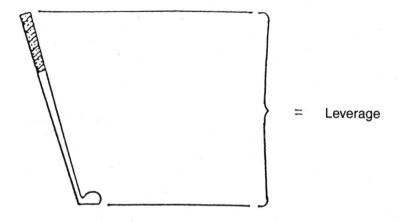

Figure 8–6 An example of leverage.

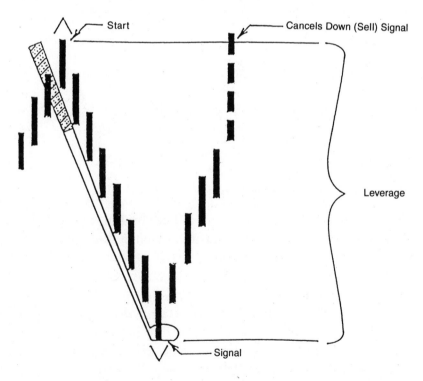

Figure 8–7 Leverage in the market.

141

TAKING ACTION

Trading the fractal is an easy way to make sure you are trading in the direction of the market momentum. When any market makes a directional move, it builds up momentum. This momentum is like a rolling ball that continues to roll until it meets resistance that has more power than the momentum of the ball. The initiating fractal tells traders which way the market river is flowing. It virtually guarantees being included in any significant trend move.

Remember that we are looking for a specific fractal formation that consists of two adjacent fractals in opposite directions. This sets up a fractal start and a fractal signal. If the fractal signal is triggered, we go in that direction. A fractal stop generally occurs two fractals back in the opposite direction, or if a buy/sell signal is created in the opposite direction. In the first case, we would have a stop. In the second case, we would have a stop-and-reverse signal.

If you determine you are in a trend run, you will maximize your profits by using the regular trailing stop (two fractals back in the opposite direction). If you determine you are in a bracketed market, you may choose to exit or stop and reverse on a thumb signal, described in the next section.

LOOKING INSIDE THE FRACTAL

Trading the fractals will guarantee that you will never be left out of any significant trend. This offers tremendous benefit because most of your trading profits will be made in trending markets. Trading only the initiating fractal can be consistently profitable. The downside, however, is that most traders give back a portion of their profits in bracketed or range-bound markets. We can improve on our profitability by going inside the fractal to get a better trade location. That also permits an earlier entry into any new trend.

The Profitunity Research Group spent three years of research going inside the fractal in an attempt to better understand the internal dynamics involved. We were able to break the code that indicates whether a change in trend is likely to be one that will start a new trend or one that will stay in the previous trading range.

Looking at Figure 8–8, we want to know whether there are any differences between points a and points b, c, and d that could give us trustworthy information telling us to buy before the breakout is obvious to other traders. Points a, b, c, and d are all fractals.

I suggest that you find a rubber band—a learning device for how to trade this technique.

Place the rubber band securely around your *right* thumb to represent the bottom of the thumb bar. It must be the right thumb, even if you are left-handed. Next, bend your ring finger and your little finger on the right hand down so that only your thumb, index finger, and middle finger are still outstretched, as in Figure 8–9.

We call this a "setup" for a possible fractal. To produce the full fractal, we must have two following bars with highs that are lower than the middle-finger high.

To place a thumb trade, you must have the three-bar setup. Each of these three bars must have a higher high *and* a higher low than the previous "finger"/bar (Figure 8–10). Inside bars

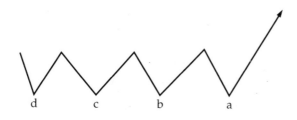

Figure 8–8   Bracketed into a trending market.

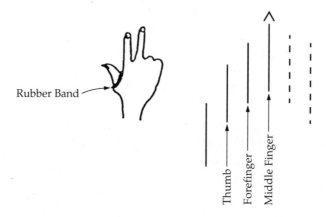

Figure 8–9   Right hand with rubber band.

cannot count as fingers because they do not have both a higher high and a higher low. It may take more than a three-bar sequence to create this setup if you have inside bars. Remember, the only ones you count are those that have higher highs *and* higher lows than the previous finger.

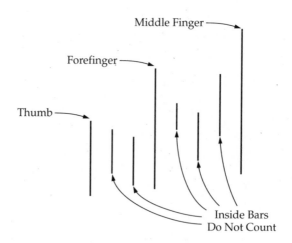

Figure 8–10   Thumb trade "setup."

The next criterion is that two of the three fingers/bars must be a squat or a green or any combination of squats and greens. In other words, two of the three bars must have increasing volume compared to the immediately previous bar.

Once you have this setup, you put in an order to sell one tick below the bottom of the thumb bar. What happens next?

If the market continues to move up and produces a higher thumb sell, you move your sell stop up (Figure 8–11).

If the market moves down and triggers your stop, you immediately place a stop and reverse to go long at the top of the middle finger, which is now a regular initiating up fractal signal. Your risk is from the bottom of the thumb bar (the placement of the rubber band) to the top of the middle finger (Figure 8–12).

This thumb trade technique will get you into the market at a much better trade location in a bracketed market. We call this area the "double duty dollar area" because we get a better trade location and we have less potential risk and more potential profit.

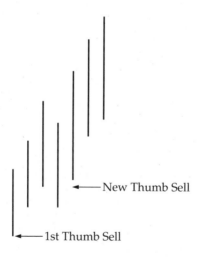

New Thumb Sell

1st Thumb Sell

Figure 8–11   Thumb trades move up with new highs.

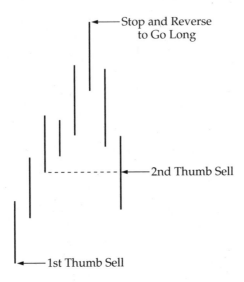

Stop and Reverse
to Go Long

2nd Thumb Sell

1st Thumb Sell

Figure 8–12   Where to place a stop and reverse if a thumb trade is triggered.

Figures 8–13 and 8–14 give a condensed description of the various forms of fractals, air bags (two-bar reversal), and thumb trades.

Figures 8–15 through 8–19 are some examples of trading simple fractals on a short time frame. Note that fractals can work equally well on longer-term time frames.

The chapter concludes with questions that will indicate your present understanding of Level Two, the Advanced Beginner in trading.

REVIEW QUESTIONS

1. How do you identify a fractal? List the essential characteristics that any fractal must contain.

2. Describe and locate the fractal start.

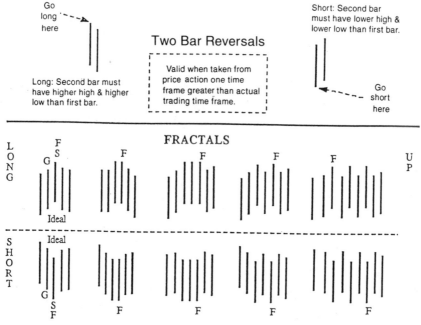

A five- (or more) bar sequence where the center bar (or group of bars) is preceded and followed by two lower bar highs for long signals or two higher lows for short signals. Bar lows have no significance on up fractals and bar highs have no significance on down fractals.

A series of three or more bars that have progressively higher highs and higher lows for short signals or lower lows and lower highs for long signals. In the thumb grouping, there must be at least one squat and one green bar. If one (or both) of these is missing, the thumb signal is considered weak.

F = Fractal   S = Squat   G = Green

Figure 8–13   Key formation definitions.

- *Hump = five-fingered boogie = fractal* (All three of these terms refer to the same formation)
- What happens when a *fractal* in one direction is followed by a *fractal* in the opposite direction is always an Elliott wave of some degree.
- A *fractal* is always a change in behavior. It is displayed as a minimum of five consecutive bars where the high (low) bar has two preceding bars and two following bars whose highs (low) are lower than the highest (lowest) bar.
- One way to trade the *fractal* is: whenever the market exceeds the outside extreme (*high* on *up fractals* and *low* on *down fractals*), "go with" the outside direction/*fractal* point.
- When opposite *fractals* form where neither extreme formation's bars overlap the other, a *hump (fractal)* signal is created. The first occurring *fractal* is called the *hump start* and the second *fractal* is the *hump signal.*

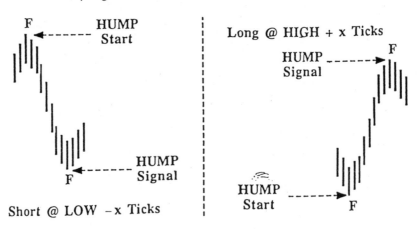

Figure 8–14   Fractal formations and signals.

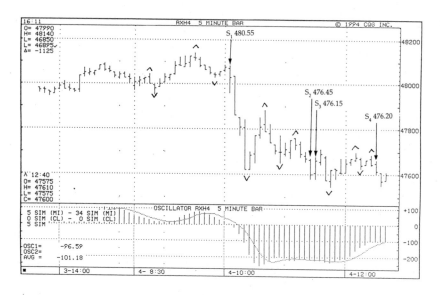

Figure 8–15 Trading simple fractal on 5-minute bars—
February 4, 1994.

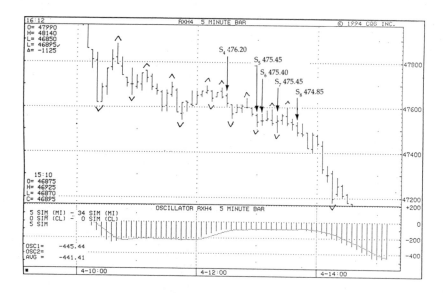

Figure 8–16 Trading simple fractal on 5-minute bars—
February 4, 1994.

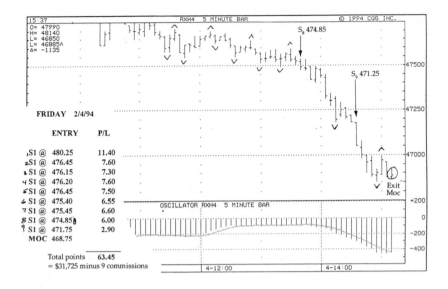

Figure 8–17 Trading simple fractal on 5-minute bars—
February 4, 1994.

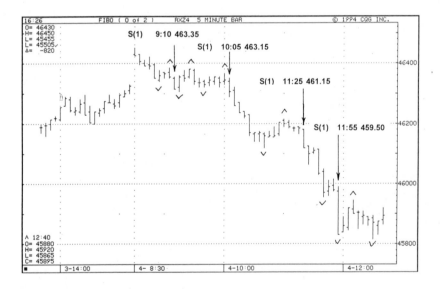

Figure 8–18 Trading simple fractal on 5-minute bars—
October 4, 1994.

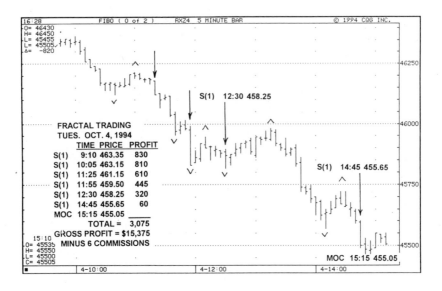

Figure 8–19 Trading simple fractal on 5-minute bars—
October 4, 1994.

3. Describe and locate the fractal signal.

4. Describe and locate the fractal stop.

5. When do you call a broker to put in a fractal trade?

6. What is the purpose of the responsive fractal (thumb trade)?

7. Describe how the thumb trade must be more "pristine" than a regular fractal.

8. What is the primary purpose of trading the thumb trade?

9. Describe the different exit strategies when trading in a trend move versus trading in a bracketed (range-bound) market.

9

Level Three:
The Competent Trader

The chief object of education is not to learn but to unlearn.

G. K. Chesterton

GOAL: TO GAIN THE ABILITY TO READ THE MARKET ACCURATELY AND KNOW THE RESPONSES THAT WILL MAXIMIZE RETURN ON INVESTMENT. THIS REQUIRES LEARNING TO USE PROFITUNITY PLANNED TRADING™ AND PREPARING TO USE PROFITUNITY TRADING PARTNER™.

We are now entering the third level in our journey to Level Five. A pianist at this level is able to play a written piece of music perfectly. This requires reading and recognizing the instructions given on the sheet music and translating them by touching the right keys at the correct speeds and timing and with the instructed amount of force. This level is accomplished because the pianist has put in the time needed for research, study, and practice, practice, practice.

However, a *competent* pianist will never be asked to play in Carnegie Hall. The Holiday Inn, maybe, but not Carnegie Hall.

At this level, one can make a living playing the piano but is not yet world class. The difference between Level Three and Level Four is that at Level Four one not only reads the music but adds or contributes something from within. A pianist at the competent level is actually a human "player piano," and "player pianos" don't collect money for tickets. Most of the pieces programmed into mechanical player pianos are fast, ragtime, or march music—each selection has a definite beat. Compositions by Brahms, Beethoven, Debussy, or Pachabel are rarely rolled through player pianos because the instrument cannot convey the music's inner "feeling."

The same analogy holds true for trading. At Level Two, the trader is making money consistently on a one-contract basis. At Level Three, trading multiple contracts, the trader should be able to double the percentage return on investment (ROI) made at Level Two by varying the volume of the trades. Level Three permits the trader to be maximally invested where there is the least risk and minimally invested where there is the greatest risk. Level Three traders are competent but do not yet know how to put *themselves* into the market. They understand the "underlying and usually unseen structure of the market" but may not yet see the relationship between that structure and the underlying and usually unseen structure of their own personality. We'll get deeply into that area in Level Four. For now, let's work at achieving competency.

PROFITUNITY PLANNED TRADING

The following material provides the best systematic approach to taking money from the market that we have seen in over 35 years of trading.* To follow this method, you must first decide what is to be your trading horizon. What time frame is most

*I am indebted to Robert Balan (1989) for the initial idea of this type of asset allocation.

comfortable with your style of trading? This approach works with all times frames, but it becomes a bit cumbersome with intraday trading. In general, the longer-term time frame incurs less overhead in commission and transaction costs and gathers less "static" from news items and other temporary aberrations in the market. In the final analysis, most traders are more profitable on a relatively longer time frame.

The following outline is our approach for trading through a complete sequence of the Elliott wave, consisting of a five-wave impulse move and a three-wave corrective move. Assume that the market has shown a clear five-wave pattern down, with the appropriate ratios, and has an appropriate "look or fit" to the wave formation.

Finding Point Zero, the End of a Tradable Trend

The first and most vital knowledge we can have about the market is the end of a trend in our trading time frame. Let's follow the various traders' behavior at a typical end-of-trend action in the market. In Figure 9–1, we can assume from the price formation that traders who are short at point d are happy; they are in profit territory. They most likely sold the breakout at point c or

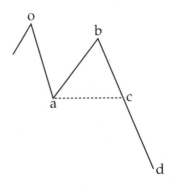

Figure 9–1 Traders getting short.

sold a pullback from around point b. Regardless of their method of entry, they are happy because they are gaining profit. At this point, probably no more than 20 percent of the traders looking at this market are in the trade. All the rest are wishing they were in and saying to themselves, "If the market gives me a pullback, I will get short."

The market does indeed give them a pullback, and more traders get short. Again, they get short on the pullback at point e or the breakout down at point f in Figure 9–2. In the total population of traders watching this market, we have a larger group of happy traders. The traders who entered at points b and c are very happy; they have lots of profit. Those who entered at points e and f are happy because they too are making profits. There is still a large group of traders who are watching but haven't yet taken action. They are giving themselves hell because they have missed four selling opportunities. They are saying to themselves, "If the market just gives me another pullback, I'm in there, buddy!"

The market becomes very kindly and does move up from point g to point h (Figure 9–3). To this last group of traders who are still not short, this pullback from point g to point h looks like the two previous pullbacks (from a to b and from d

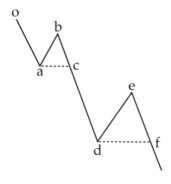

Figure 9–2 Short entry of the second group of traders.

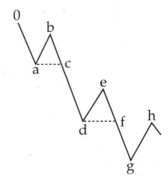

Figure 9–3 The entry of the weak shorts.

to e) which are producing nice profits. This last group of traders go short around point h, earning the label "weak shorts" because they are in late and have little staying power.

What the weak shorts or constant losers don't see is that 0-a is wave 1, b-d is wave 3, and e-g is wave 5. What they see as an opportune pullback is really the first initial thrust of the new trend going in the opposite direction. They generally will get stopped out when the price goes above point h.

They do not see that point 0 through point g is a five-wave Elliott sequence. To be winning traders, we need a technique to (1) give us high confidence when a trend is over and (2) present us with a "market-determined" technique for maximizing our profits in the new upcoming Elliott wave sequence. We call this end of a significant trend *Point Zero*. Once we are satisfied that this is Point Zero, we plan a trading campaign to maximize our profits throughout the upcoming Elliott wave.

Five Magic Bullets That Will Kill Most Trends

The key to "making a killing" in the market lies in the ability to know when a trend is over and when the next trend is starting. In Chapter 7, we introduced five magic bullets and said that when they are present, the odds are heavily in favor of a trend's being over. These bullets are:

1. Divergence. There must be a divergence between wave 3 and wave 5 (see Figure 9–4). If the market is going down, the price at the end of wave 5 must be lower than the bottom of wave 3 and the Profitunity oscillator must be higher at the end of wave 5 than it was at the end of wave 3.

2. Price in the target zone. (The technique for projecting this target zone is found in Chapter 7.)

3. A fractal at the bottom (top).

4. A squat bar in one of the three bottom (top) bars.

5. A shift in momentum from down to up (up to down, in a bull market). (See Chapter 7.)

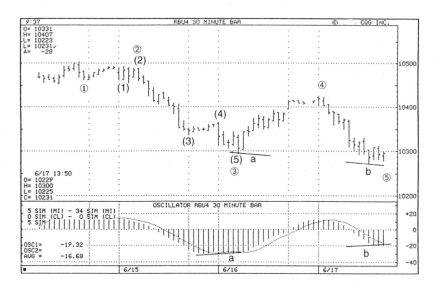

Figure 9–4 Divergence between wave 3 and wave 5.

Once these five magic bullets show up, you assume that this is a Point Zero. Your situation would be:

1. There is divergence between wave 3 and wave 5.

2. The price is in the target zone. This divergence is measured in a time frame in which the Elliott wave you are counting occupies between 100 and 140 bars.

3. A fractal has developed.

4. A Squat bar is on one of the three bottommost (topmost) bars.

5. There is a change in direction of momentum as measured on the Profitunity 5/34/5 MACD.

When you see all five of these bullets, you can begin your count with confidence.

At Point Zero, we expect a sharp rally of the bottom (Figure 9–5). We move down at least one significant time frame. If the

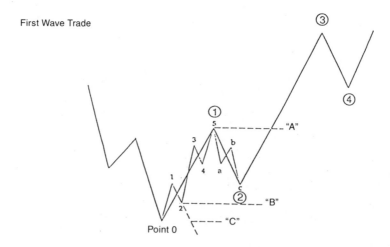

Figure 9–5   Trading the first wave of an Elliott wave sequence.

trading time frame is a daily bar, we would examine a 60- or possibly a 30-minute bar. We are looking for a smaller degree five-wave impulse in the new direction. As this rally begins to lose steam (usually with an up fractal) and starts to pull back, we want to be ready to place our first trade in this sequence. Our assumption at this point is that a possible impulse wave up has begun. If that is not the case, we are in some sort of corrective mode and our strategy must take account of this possibility. We assume that this is the end of a wave 1 up (Figure 9–5).

As this first pullback from the up move starts, we place our first buy. If we cannot watch the market on a short-term basis, we place our order somewhere between a 50 percent and a 62 percent pullback (point "B" in Figure 9–5). If we are able to watch the market as this develops, we will go to an even shorter-term chart and look for five waves in wave c of wave 2. On the smaller-term chart, we look for exactly the same signals we were searching for to determine the end of a trend. Wave 2 represents a shorter time interval. If we are watching those five magic bullets form in wave c of wave 2, we can make an even more precise entry, taking more profit and less risk.

If we are trading multiple contracts (assume our maximum trading capacity is 10 contracts), we want to place an order to buy three contracts (or 30 percent or our maximum number of contracts available for this trading sequence). As soon as we are filled, we want to determine two things: (1) where to protect against excessive losses and (2) where to take profits. Our first obligation is to cut losses, so we will place a stop and reverse to go short just below the low at Point Zero (point "C" in Figure 9–5). We place an order to sell five contracts (half of our maximum). Our logic for this stop and reverse is that if the price goes below what we thought was Point Zero, our count is wrong and what we had assumed was an impulsive wave up is, in fact, a reaction to a continuing down trend.

Being wrong can often prove to be as profitable as being right. If we are clearly wrong in our count, we should not just get out; rather, we should reverse to the opposite direction. The only time to get out is when you don't know where you are in the market movement or you are waiting for good trade location. Here, we place an order to go short two-thirds of our long position. That means that if we are long three contracts, we must place an order to sell five to be net short two, which is two-thirds of our long position. Our experience in actual trading has been that we can almost always make enough profit on this short to overcome any loss on the long side.

If we are wrong in being on the long side, we should latch on to the breakout trade on the down side. Because this is clearly a breakout to the down side, our stop would be two fractals back in the opposite (long) direction.

Assuming that we did not get stopped out one tick below Point Zero, we believe that we are in the beginning of a wave 1, which should include a five-wave pattern visible on a smaller time frame. Let's be clear here: nobody "knows" this is a wave 1. It could be a corrective wave a. No problem; our strategy will take care of that possibility also.

As the market nears our larger-degree wave ① (and our smaller-degree wave 5, inside of wave ①; see Figure 9–5), we want to bank some of our profits. We are long three contracts, so we sell two. We do this for two reasons: (1) to take some money to the bank and (2) to leave one contract long in case our target is wrong and the market continues up (at least one contract will continue to give us profits).

By using the methods described above (the five magic bullets) and applying Fibonacci expansion ratios (discussed earlier), we can calculate that the end of this five-wave pattern will make a larger wave ① (point "A" in Figure 9–5).

We have now taken profits on two contracts, are still holding one long, and are awaiting an opportunity to add to our long position on an appropriate pullback. As this larger-degree wave ② pulls back to between 50 percent and 62 percent, we will initiate our second trade: we will attempt to buy near the bottom of wave 2 (point "D" in Figure 9–6). We will verify the bottom of wave 2 by a down fractal and a squat bar on one of the three lowest bars in this wave. In addition, we go to a smaller time frame to count the five waves inside wave c of wave ②. At this predetermined point, we would buy five contracts, giving us a total of six contracts (counting the one we left on at the end of the smaller-degree wave 1).

Once again, it is time to protect and plan where to take profits. Our stop and reverse will remain the same, just below Point Zero (point "C" in Figure 9–6). If this point is hit, we will sell ten contracts, leaving us net short four contracts. Using the same reasoning as for the first trade, we would need only a relatively small movement to recoup our losses on the six long contracts. If this point is hit, it most likely indicates that our analysis is wrong and our anticipated bullishness should turn bearish. What we had first analyzed as the top of wave 1 is

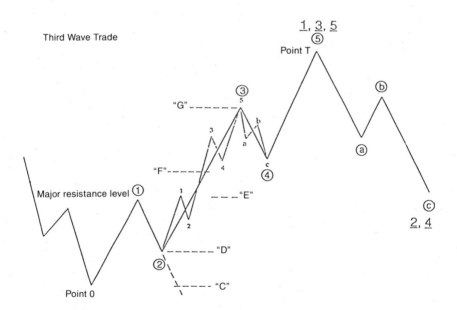

Figure 9–6   Trading the third wave of an Elliott wave sequence.

more likely the end of a larger-degree wave 2 or wave 4, which means much more on the downside. After the reverse, we are in tune with the immediate trend.

If, as expected, the market moves higher, we must plan to extract some more profits (the name of this game) from the market. The next critical point in this campaign is where the young wave ③ equals the length of wave ① (point "F" in Figure 9–6). At this point, we still have our order to sell ten contracts just below our Point Zero. If the market stalls here and retraces past the top of wave 1 (point "E" in Figure 9–6), we want out altogether so we sell six contracts. We do this by canceling our standing order to sell ten contracts just below Point Zero and placing an order to sell six contracts one tick below the top of what we think is wave ①. Our logic here is that our expected count is not unfolding and we should get out just until the market has time to clear the wave-count picture.

If the prices continue upward to where the emerging wave ③ is 10 percent longer than wave ①, we are most likely in a real wave ③. We want to go "whole hog" so we buy four more contracts, giving us our maximum of ten longs. This is the point to be maximally long and most aggressive: this wave gives the most profit per unit of time and contains the least risk. We also want to place a stop for the additional four contracts where we now have the order to sell six—just below the top of wave 1. If the market comes one tick below the top of what we think is wave 1, we want to be out of the market completely.

Our thinking behind this is:

1. Wave 4 should not come below the top of wave 1.

2. If it does, it destroys our current count—we don't know where we are and therefore should be out.

As the price rallies and we get totally on board, we want to calculate the most probable completion point for wave ③ (point

"G" in Figure 9–6). We do this by again using our five magic bullets that kill most trends. When we have used the bullets and the price reaches our calculated goal, we sell seven of the ten contracts. Our reasoning is exactly the same as when we sold two contracts at the top of wave ①. We want to bank the majority of the profits and stay in a minor position, in case the current movement proves to be an extended wave. At this point, the 5/34 oscillator should be considerably higher than its peak at the top of wave ①. If that happens, we are in a good situation. We are still making profit on 30 percent of our total, and we have already taken a sizable amount of money to the bank. This is the best of all trading worlds.

Now is the time to allow wave ④ to retrace. We watch this retracement very carefully for clues on when to reenter on the long side. If wave a of wave ④ breaks down into five waves, we normally expect a zigzag correction and much lower prices. If wave a is only three waves, we normally expect a flat, irregular, or triangle correction. When the 5/34 oscillator goes below the zero line, the minimum requirements for wave ④ have been met. It is important to remember that going below zero does *not* indicate that wave ④ is over, only that it has *met the minimum requirements*. It is, however, time to start looking for a place to take advantage of the upcoming wave ⑤. Wave ④ will also contain a minimum of two down fractals and will end in a squat bar on one or more of the three lowest bars. Another good indicator is that it usually ends in the area of the previous wave 4 of a lesser degree (the fourth wave inside of wave ③).

The criterion for determining how many contracts to enter at this point (bottom of wave ④) is the ratio of the length of wave ③ to wave ①. If wave ③ is equal to or longer than 1.62 times wave ①, it is probably an extended wave ③, and wave ⑤ will be relatively shorter. In that case, we would add to our three long contracts another three, giving us a total of six contracts to hold through wave ⑤. We would put this buy between 38 percent and 50 percent retracement of wave ③ (point "H" in

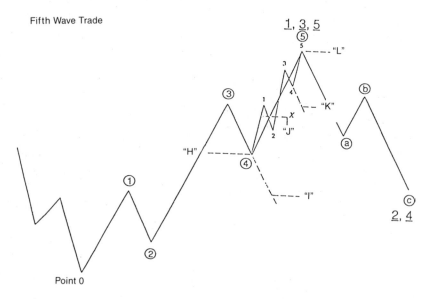

Fifth Wave Trade

Figure 9–7   Trading the fifth wave of an Elliott wave sequence.

Figure 9–7). If wave ③ is less than 1.62 times as long as wave 1, we would buy five contracts, giving us a total of eight contracts long. The reason for this decision is: usually, one of the three impulse waves in a five-wave series is an "extended" wave, and this extension most often occurs in wave ③. Sometimes, however, it does occur in wave ⑤, even more rarely, it may be in wave ①. If wave ③ is not an extended wave, the probability is that wave ⑤ will extend. This justifies our putting on an additional two contracts.

Our initial stop for these six (or eight) contracts would be at the top of wave ① (point "I" in Figure 9–7). We would sell enough contracts to be out of the market.

If the anticipated wave 5 continues upward, it verifies our premise and wave count. The critical point here is when the rally reaches a 62 percent retracement of the down move in wave 4 (point "J" in Figure 9–7). if the market rallies above this point, it is highly unlikely that a larger move down will occur, and we need to think about taking profits again. We project the end of a five-wave sequence that makes up the larger-degree wave 5. At this point, we sell all our remaining long contracts and go flat the market (point "L" in Figure 9–7).

Trading the Corrective Waves

We basically follow the same logic in trading the three-wave corrective pattern. We watch the first down move, which is usually dynamic, and sell on a 50 percent to 62 percent retracement upward (Figure "M" in Figure 9–8), placing a stop and reverse to go net long just above the top of wave ⑤ (point "O" in Figure 9–8). If wave a turns into a five-wave sequence, we expect a zigzag correction and a deep move back down.

At the calculated end of wave a, we buy back two contracts and leave one short in case the market continues downward

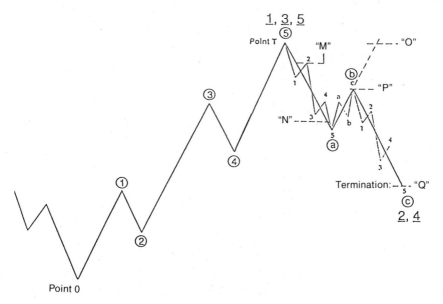

Figure 9–8 Trading the corrective wave of an Elliott wave sequence.

(point "N" in Figure 9–8). We then calculate that with a 38–50 percent (point "P" in Figure 9–8) retracement back up, we could sell three more units, expecting wave c to have a wave 3 personality on the down side. We place a stop and reverse above the top of wave 5 (point "O" in Figure 9–8) for seven contracts, giving us a new long of three contracts if the market moves that high. Concluding this sequence, we calculate the projected end of wave 5 of wave c (point "Q" in Figure 9–8). At that point, we cover all shorts and wait for the next movement of the market to unfold.

Examples of Profitunity Planned Trading

Swiss Franc Weekly

This is an example of longer-term trading, which has the advantage of little intensive monitoring of the market while cutting down the overhead spent on commission cost. A disadvantage is that the stops must be further away, with more risk. However, one can pinpoint the Point Zero, where there is a minimum of risk. This was the Profitunity Trading Group's first excursion into trading the weekly chart. Before then, our longest term of actual trading was based on the daily charts.

Notice the monthly chart in Figure 9–9. We used this chart to locate what we surmised to be the bottom of a wave 4 in May 1989. During June 1989, FNN (now CNBC-FNN) asked me to appear on a panel with five other traders, including two FNN staff members, to discuss the future direction of the American dollar. The other five panel members all agreed that the dollar was very bullish and should go up. I was the lone dissenter, basing my thinking on the wave count in the Swiss franc, Deutsche mark, and Japanese yen. I predicted that the Swiss franc would top 8000 in its next move. My statement generated snickers and outright laughter from the other panel members. At this point, I knew I had made not only a financial commitment but also an ego commitment.

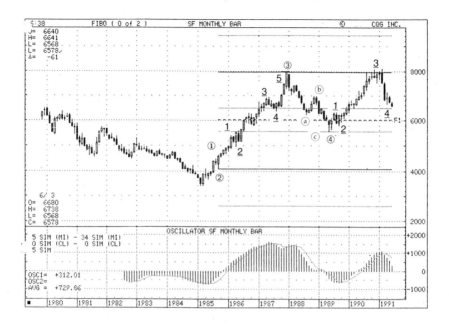

Figure 9–9 Monthly Swiss franc chart showing the end of a wave 4.

My trading plan was to apply Profitunity Planned Trading (PPT) to wave 5 on the monthly chart. My Point Zero on the weekly chart was the bottom of wave 4 on the monthly chart. Figure 9–10 is the weekly chart of the Swiss franc that we actually traded. Let's go through the exact trades and why they were placed where they were. Our trading schedule called for a maximum of ten contracts in this particular campaign.

Point Zero happened on May 22, 1989, and was evidenced by a clear five-wave sequence down on the smaller-time-frame daily chart plus a down fractal with a squat day on one of the three bottom bars.

It is important to emphasize that I *assumed* I was looking at a Point Zero. In the beginning stages of a PPT sequence, one never knows whether the correct point has been labeled as Point Zero. Therein lies the beauty of the PPT: there is always a

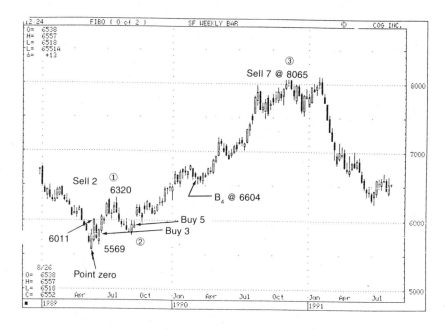

Figure 9–10 Weekly Swiss franc chart used in the PPT strategy.

contingency plan if the count is incorrect. My Point Zero was followed, as expected, by a sharp upturn that ended at 6011 on June 5, 1989. By going to a smaller time frame (dailies and 60-minute charts), a complete five-wave sequence could be counted.

At this point, I calculated a 62 percent retracement and put in an order to buy three contracts at 5736 or better, with a stop and reverse to go short five contracts at Point Zero (5569). The total risk at this point was 167 points or $2,087.50 per contract (a total of $6,262.50 for the three contracts). The low of this pullback was 5630 or an exposure of $1,175 per contract.

The market then started up in a small-degree wave 3 and completed five waves up (much clearer on the daily chart) at 6320. Using a down fractal and the squat, I sold two of the three long contracts for a profit of 584 points per contract or a total closed-out profit of $14,600. This left me long one contract, in case this turned out to be an extended wave 1. The end of the fifth wave of a larger-degree wave 1 happened on July 31, 1989.

I then calculated a 62 percent retracement of this larger wave 1:

$$6320 - 5569 = 751 \times .62 = 465$$

This result was subtracted from the high (6320), and I put in an order to buy five contracts at 5854. This order was hit on August 28, 1989. The market continued down to a low of 5778 on September 11, 1989.

Then the market started moving up in earnest for a larger-degree wave 3. I was long six contracts (or 60 percent of my total position limit). The length of wave 1 was 751 points, so I added 10 percent to that total and added four more contracts, for a limit position of ten contracts at 6604. My stop at this point, for all ten, as 6320, or the top of wave 1.

My current positions were then:

Long one contract at 5736

Long five contracts at 5854

Long four contracts at 6604

If stopped out at the top of wave 1, I would have the following results:

Long one contract at 5736	+ $7,300
Long five contracts at 5834	+ 29,125
Long four contracts at 6604	− 14,200

I had a closed-out profit of $14,600 from the first two contracts and a minimum profit of $22,225 from the other ten.

169

Wave 3 turned out to be an extended wave 3 with no fractal reversals until November 19, 1990. On that date, I took profits at approximately 100 points from the high at 7965 on seven of the ten long positions. I had the following closed-out profits (not counting commissions):

Long one contract at 5736	+ $ 27,802.50
Long five contracts at 5854	+ 131,937.50
Long one (of four) contracts at 6604	+ 17,012.50
Plus the first closed-out trade	+ 22,225.00
Total closed out profit	$198,977.50

I was still long three contracts from 6604. On the weekly chart, we seemed to be in a wave b test of wave 4. I was awaiting a minimum of two down fractals and/or a pullback to the 6650–7200 area. Wave 3 was *more than 1.62 times as long at wave 1,* so I added only three more long contracts.

On April 29, 1991, the Swiss franc retraced back to a low of 6666, which was almost exactly a 62 percent retracement. (Only one out of eight times will a wave 4 retrace more than 62 percent.) I also had what appeared to be a five-wave count for wave c of wave 4. Therefore, I bought three more contracts on April 29, on the first hourly up fractal, at 6711. My stop for all six contracts was 6630. On June 9, I was stopped out at 6630 for a total loss on the six contracts of $4,125. Subtracting this amount from my previous profits gave me a total profit of $194,100 for this series of trades.

This may not be the mother of all trades, but two points are significant here. This entire series of trades could have been completed with a $10,000 account, without ever margining more than 50 percent of that account. Only five trades were placed in a period of approximately 18 months. This type of trading can be done by anyone, no matter what other professional and time obligations must be met. One literally could have placed a trade, gone on a cruise, returned to place another trade, and repeated that procedure five times while paying for the cruises from profits.

Profitunity Planned Trading—Shorter Term

March—Soybeans

In this series of trades, looking first at the daily chart (Figure 9–11), we saw that there was a Point Zero that met all our requirements on September 12, 1991, with a high of 668½. It then proceeded to move down, in a five-wave sequence on the hourly chart, to 654½. (This was more clearly visible on a 60-minute chart.) Following the specific techniques of Profitunity Planned Trading, we would have sold three contracts at a 62 percent retracement, which was 663 with a stop and reverse to

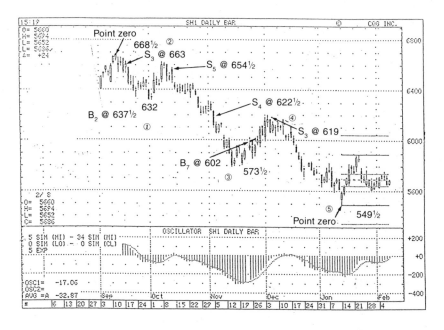

Figure 9–11 Tracking soybean traders on a daily chart.

171

go long five contracts at 668½. (Our risk at this point for the three contracts would have been $1,375, or $458 per contract.) The beans did move down, tracing out a clearly defined five-wave sequence with a squat on the bottom fractal at 632. Assuming we had waited for the first hourly up fractal signal, the worst we could have done was buy back two contracts at 637½, giving us a closed-out profit of $1,275 per contract, or $2,550 for both contracts. This would have left us short one contract from 663, with a stop at 668½.

From the Elliott wave count, the fractal, and the Profitunity windows, we might have concluded that this most likely was a wave 1 down and expected at least a 50–62 percent retracement. Wave 1 down was 36½ cents and ended at 632, so we would have had a resting sell order to an additional five contracts at 654¾ or better, with a stop at 668½. We would have been filled because the market went back up to 662½ but did not reach the stop at 668½. From there, the market began moving down with third-wave enthusiasm through the last of October and into the first half of November. If we had added the final four contracts at 110 percent of wave 1 (622½), we would have then been short a whole load with stops at the bottom of wave 1 (632).

We would then have had a closed-out profit of $2,550 on the first two contracts. Our position would have been:

Short one contract at 663

Short five contracts at 654¾

Short four contracts at 622½

Our next step would have been to calculate the end of wave 3 using the five magic bullets explained earlier in this chapter. There were five countable waves with a fractal and a squat on November 11, with a low of 578½. In the worst outcome, we would have bought back seven contracts on the daily up fractal signal on November 23 at 602. Our balance sheet would have been:

Short two contracts with closed-out profits	+ $ 2,550.00
Short one contract from 663 (61 × $50)	+ 3,050.00
Short five contracts from 654¾ (52.75 × $50)	+ 13,187.50
Short one contract from 622½ (20.5 × $50)	+ 1,025.00
Total closed profit	$17,262.50

We would still have been short three contracts from 622½ with a stop at 631.

Next, we would have sold a 38 to 50 percent retracement of wave 3. Because wave 3 was more than 1.62 times as long as wave 1, we would have sold three more contracts at 619, with the stop for these at 631 also.

To end this sequence of trades, we would have calculated the end of wave 5 and found it to be 561—the exit on all shorts. The balance sheet would now have $17,262.50 from earlier trades in this sequence plus:

Short three contracts from 622½ (61.5 × 3 × $50)	$9,225.00
Short three contracts from 619 (58 × 3 × $50)	8,700.00

Total closed-out profit from September 12 through January 9 would have been $35,187.50 in slightly less than four months. This trading program could have been handled with a $15,000 account, without ever margining over 50 percent of the account equity.

The two examples in this section should give you an idea of the power of letting the market dictate your asset allocation. The added factor of following the market's leadership is low-stress trading, which we address in Chapters 11 and 12.

SUMMARY

In this chapter, we have examined the best asset allocation plan we have found in 35 years of actively trading the markets. All the allocations are based on market information rather than derivative opinions. The design extracts the maximum amount of profit with the least amount of risk. It is easy and does not require continuous monitoring if you are trading on a daily basis.

At this Level Three of trading, our aim is to maximize our ROI with multiple contracts, as opposed to Level Two, where our aim was to make consistent profits on a one-contract basis. It is not unusual for traders at Level Two to double their *percentage* return on investments by varying the volume of their trades. This allows them to be maximally invested where there is the least risk and minimally invested where there is the greatest risk.

REVIEW QUESTIONS

1. What is the importance of always using Profitunity Planned Trading (PPT)?

2. What are the advantages of using PPT techniques rather than trading a comfortable volume of contracts using fractal trading techniques?

3. What percentage of your total capacity of contracts should you place on the first trade?

4. Where would you stop and reverse the first trade?

5. What are the five magic bullets?

6. Why do you exit two-thirds of your position at the top of wave 1?

7. What is the reasoning behind being fully invested when wave 3 equals 110 percent of wave 1?

8. How do you decide how many contracts to trade during wave 5?

9. What do you do at the end of wave 5?

———10———

Profitunity Trading Partner

Every divided kingdom falls, so every mind divided between many studies confounds and saps itself.

Leonardo da Vinci

GOALS:

1. **TO INCORPORATE THE SKILLS LEARNED IN LEVELS ONE, TWO, AND THREE INTO AN EASY-TO-USE CHECKLIST THAT WILL IMPROVE TRADING EFFICIENCY.**
2. **TO BE ABLE TO COMPLETELY ANALYZE A MARKET IN 10 SECONDS OR LESS.**

One of the perennial problems all traders face is how to condense the enormous amount of material the market is putting out each minute into an easy-to-understand decision-making format. A concurrent problem is how to put this material into a form that will automatically prioritize the information so that trading decisions are made in a responsible profit-making sequence.

Figure 10–1 is a sample worksheet of our Profitunity Trading Partner. This is the simplest, easiest-to-use, most profit-producing and time-saving method of keeping market analysis

PROFITUNITY WorkSheet   Date ____/____/____

①   ③   ④   ②   ⑤

Market-Mo. Settlement		2-Bar Reverse	Hump Signals	Thumb Signals	Rhythm TWR ¦ MACD	Current Trades	Proposed Trades	Open Equity	Open Close	$/point
ED -	BUY								6:20	$25
Last:	SELL								13:00	
BD -	BUY								6:20	$1,000
Last:	SELL								13:00	
GC -	BUY								6:20	$10
Last:	SELL								12:30	
SI -	BUY								6:25	$5
Last:	SELL								12:25	
CP -	BUY								7:25	$2.50
Last:	SELL								12:00	
SU -	BUY								8:00	$11.20
Last:	SELL								11:43	
CL -	BUY								7:45	$10
Last:	SELL								13:10	
HO -	BUY								7:50	$4.20
Last:	SELL								13:10	
S -	BUY								8:30	$50
Last:	SELL								12:15	
BO -	BUY								8:30	$6
Last:	SELL								12:15	
C -	BUY								8:30	$50
Last:	SELL								12:15	
W -	BUY								8:30	$50
Last:	SELL								12:15	
CT -	BUY								8:30	$5
Last:	SELL								12:40	
SF -	BUY								6:20	$12.50
Last:	SELL								13:00	
DM -	BUY								6:20	$12.50
Last:	SELL								13:00	
JY -	BUY								6:20	$12.50
Last:	SELL								13:00	
CF -	BUY								7:15	$3.75
Last:	SELL								11:58	
CC -	BUY								7:30	$10.00
Last:	SELL								12:15	
BP -	BUY								6:20	$6.25
Last:	SELL								13:00	

Figure 10–1   Profitunity trading partner worksheet.

on track that we have seen in 35+ years of trading. The circled numbers on the various columns in Figure 10–1 indicate the order in which the worksheet is filled out. Assume that you are doing your market analysis after a vacation and are coming in absolutely "clean" of any previous information. You are starting from scratch.

The first vertical column contains abbreviations for the commodities you are about to analyze. No month for trading is given. Using a pencil, you will note in the columns the months when the trading occurs. On each row, to the right of the commodity listings, are two rows marked "buy" and "sell." Buy and sell signals are to be entered on the appropriate lines.

THE TWO-BAR REVERSE

Let's start with the first column to the right of the commodity listings. This column is labeled at the top "2-Bar Reverse." It is important to fill in this column first.

As mentioned in Chapter 6, most traders who have left trading because they lost money have been blown out because of one or a very few *large* mistakes (losses) rather than because they were eaten up by the termite (small) losses. A trader's first and most important job is to protect the trading capital. Earlier, I used an analogy from driving. I have been driving for 45 years and have never caused a serious accident, but I have been in two accidents caused by drunken drivers. I never drink and drive. Should I then conclude that, because I am at least a decent driver, I need not spend money on extras like air bags?

I would never buy a new car *without* air bags—not to protect me from my own driving but as protection against drunk drivers. Guess what, trading fans: Sometimes the market overindulges and goes on a binge. The binge is usually caused by the market's ingesting too much surprising (intoxicating) information. Therefore, I will never buy or sell a new position without making sure that this profit potential vehicle has a good "air bag." In trading, the air bag is a two-bar reversal, but not just any two-bar reversal. It must be a two-bar reversal on a *higher time frame.*

The market can be conveniently divided into somewhat equal time intervals. The largest chart most traders view is the monthly chart. With an average of 4.3 weeks in a month, we can say that the monthly chart is a significantly higher time frame than the weekly chart, which contains only the five trading days. The daily chart usually has 4–6 hours of trading, and the hourly chart can be divided into four 15-minute or six 10-minute time periods. Thus, the market gives us at least five different time layers where the time periods above and below are approximate factors of 5. A *higher time frame* refers to a time frame that contains approximately five times the span of the current trading time frame. For example:

Monthly charts contain 4.3 weeks

Weekly charts contain 5 days

Daily charts contain 4–6 trading hours

Hourly charts contain 4 (15-min.) or (10-min.) periods

The two-bar reversal is on one significant time frame higher than whatever time period you are trading (Figure 10–2). For a more complete explanation of how to determine where the air bag should be placed, refer back to Level One (Chapter 6). If your trading time frame is the daily chart, your two-bar reversal will be on the weekly chart. If you are trading the 10-minute intraday chart, your significantly higher time frame will be the hourly chart.

If you are in a long position on the daily chart, your two-bar reversal will be on the weekly chart. Locate this point by reading the weekly chart from *right to left,* starting with the current weekly bar. Continue to the left until you find the first weekly

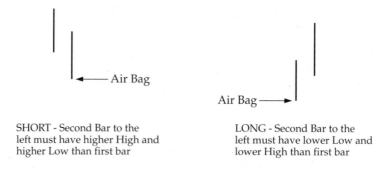

SHORT - Second Bar to the
left must have higher High and
higher Low than first bar

LONG - Second Bar to the
left must have lower Low and
lower High than first bar

Valid when taken from
price action one significant
time frame higher than
actual trading time frame

Figure 10–2   Two-bar reversals.

bar that has both a lower high and a lower low than the current
bar. *Inside bars do not count.* They do not have *both* a lower low
and a lower high (higher low and higher high). Once this point
is established (the bottom minus one tick or the top plus one
tick on the two-bar reversal bar), immediately place an air bag
stop. This is not necessarily a place to reverse (although it
could be). The purpose of this column on the Profitunity Trading Partner is to make sure that you are not long if the price
goes below the two-bar reverse low, or short if the price goes
above the two-bar reverse high. The air bag protects you from
getting killed by a weaving drunken market. That point is the
first information entered on the Profitunity Trading Partner,
and it is placed on the appropriate buy or sell row—on the buy
row if it is a two-bar up, and on the sell row if it is a two-bar
down.

RHYTHM

The next column to work with on the Profitunity Trading Partner is the column labeled "Rhythm." We use this column to

make sure that our beat or rhythm is in sync with the market. We already know that the best way to make money is to trade with the market rather than try to "buck" it. This column gives us an accurate look at the various market rhythms as we trade. It makes sure that our trading is not dancing to a fox trot while the market is playing boogie-woogie.

The science of chaos has given us overwhelming evidence that the markets are a natural process and do not follow the traditional laws of the Euclidean/Newtonian world. A natural rhythm that almost everyone has witnessed is the tides on a seashore. If you are on a beach and want to know which direction the tide is moving, you can simply stick a piece of shell or driftwood into the sand at the water's edge. After a while, the water will be either above the marker (incoming tide) or beyond the marker (outgoing tide).

If you observe the motion of the tide, you will notice that some waves are coming in with the tide and others are going out against the tide. Look even closer at the waves and you will notice that as the waves come in, some ripples on top of the waves are riding on an incoming wave and some are going out against the next incoming wave.

This is exactly how the longer-term, intermediate-term, and short-term rhythms of the markets interact. We call this the tide/wave/ripple or TWR rhythm. *The best way to monitor this market rhythm is to use a 5/13/34 moving average filter* (Figure 10–3).

The TWR information lets you know that you are in sync with the rhythms of the market. A simple formula is:

Be long any time the 5-bar average is higher than both the 13-bar and 34-bar averages.

A simple way to mark this in the Rhythm section is to place an up arrow (↑) if the 5-bar average is above both the 13-bar and the 34-bar averages. Place a down arrow (↓) if the 5-bar average

Figure 10–3 The TWR (5/13/34) moving average filter.

is below both the 13-bar and the 34-bar averages. Enter a zero as the rhythm if the 5-bar average is between the 13-bar and 34-bar averages.

We can monitor the immediate rhythm of the market even more closely by using our Elliott wave indicator, the 5/34/5 Profitunity MACD, discussed in Chapter 7. To display this MACD, I usually use a histogram to display the oscillator (which simply subtracts a 34-bar moving average from a 5-bar moving average) and a line to display the 5-bar moving average of the oscillator. (See Figure 10–4.) This gives an extremely good *immediate momentum* indicator. Whenever the histogram is higher (+1 is higher than −1, and −1 is higher than −3), the immediate momentum is up; whenever the histogram is lower, the immediate momentum is down. Your trade (long/short) should be on the histogram side of the signal line.

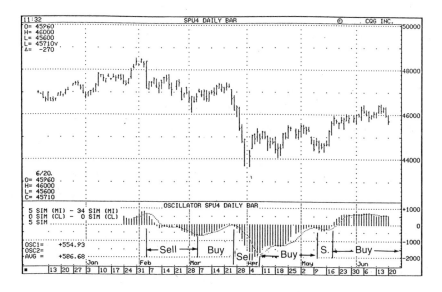

Figure 10–4   The 5/34/5 profitunity MACD.

Now let's record our observations on the Profitunity Trading Partner worksheet (Figure 10–1). We want to record both the TWR and the MACD momentum on our current trading time frame and on one significantly higher time frame. In the Rhythm column, we will use the top row (the buy row) to record the higher time frame readings and the bottom row (the sell row) to record the current trading time frame readings.

Enter the TWR reading on the left portion of the buy and sell rows and the 5/34/5 Profitunity MACD reading on the right portion of the buy and sell rows (Figure 10–5). This creates a Rhythm box that has four pieces of momentum information. The left portion will have up arrows, down arrows, or zeros, and the right portion will only have up arrows or down arrows.

The Rhythm column will give you hours of profitable fun examining all the different permutations of the arrows and

WorkSheet   Date ___

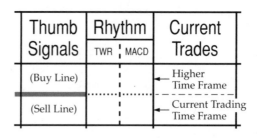

Figure 10–5   Key areas of the rhythm column.

zeros. Remember that our profession is one of speculation and as good (and highly paid) speculators we must see paradigm changes before the masses do. When a move becomes obvious to everyone, it will have all four arrows in the same direction. By then, most likely, it will be too late to climb aboard. It will definitely be too late to squeeze the maximum amount of available profit from the move.

I would want an overriding reason before I would place a new order that is not in rhythm with the lower right-hand arrow (the MACD momentum on the current trading time frame). On the other hand, if all four arrows are pointing the same way, the *greatest* trading opportunity has already been missed.

Let's review the information we have gathered so far on the Profitunity Trading Partner. We have protection (the air bag) in the form of the two-bar reversal on a significantly higher time frame. We also know more than 95 percent of all traders do, just by looking at the Rhythm column. We know where the market is in its current movement from up to down and back.

FRACTAL (HUMP) SIGNALS

The middle two columns of the worksheet (Figure 10–1) provide the boundaries within which we will trade, and our trading tools are contained in the "Hump Signals" and "Thumb Signals" columns. Our job here is simple; we are working now with only the current trading time frame. We again read from right to left (current to past bars), and we note the last fractal buy and sell signal that still contains appropriate leverage. See Chapter 8 for a full description of fractals and leverage.

THUMB SIGNALS

The next step is to note any thumb signals (see Chapter 8) and include them appropriately on the buy or sell line.

At this point, we have condensed all the necessary direct market information and have converted it into easy-to-read trading signals. To integrate this material with our current positions, we list our ongoing trades in the "Current Trades" column.

When all this information is at hand, it is time to make an executive decision. We consider our current equity and the number of positions already in the market. Are we in a Profitunity Planned Trading sequence? Where are we and what are the potentials in the Elliott wave, on both the current time frame and one significantly higher time frame?

We list our proposed trades in the "Proposed" column. To continue trading, we need only update this one sheet of paper (Figure 10–1), which is truly our "trading partner."

We make all entries in pencil. As the market progresses through the current trading time frame, we erase the space and enter the changed information. I have found, over the years, that this tactile intervention gives me a very good handle on the market's immediate personality.

In Figure 10–6, the process is condensed into an outline so that you can follow the procedural steps without rereading all the explanations.

    I. Air Bag Protection
       A. The number-one cause of accidents
          1. Who gets hurt
          2. Protecting yourself with the air bag
          3. The air bag in trading
             a. The two-bar reversal on a significantly higher time frame
          4. Not an initiating signal, but gives protection from drunken, staggering market movements
   II. Rhythms of the Market
       A. Tide/wave ripple (TWR)
          1. Looking at the market as a "natural" phenomenon
             a. 5/13/34 Moving averages
                i. If 5 is above 13 and 34, you should be *long*
                ii. If 5 is below 13 and 34, you should be *short*
                iii. If 5 is between 13 and 34, you should be out
                   (a) Indicator will be *up, down,* or *zero*
          2. Using an MACD for accurately counting Elliott waves and determining the current market momentum
             a. The three things the 5/34/5 Profitunity MACD can tell you about the Elliott wave
                i. Peak of wave 3
                   (a) Special cases of waves 3 and 5 inside of wave 3
                ii. End of a trend
                iii. When the "minimum" requirements for wave 4 have been met
             b. The same MACD can detect market momentum
                i. Take fractal signals only when this momentum indicator is in the direction of the fractal signal
                   (a) Indicator will be either up or down
  III. Locating Fractal Signals
       A. Minimum of five bars
       B. Must have current leverage
  IV. Locating Thumb Signals
       A. Minimum of three bars with higher highs and higher lows, or lower lows and lower highs
       B. At least two of the three bars must have increasing volume
       C. Inside and/or parallel bars do not count
       D. Two of the three bars musts have increasing volume, or there must be two greens, two squats, or a squat and a green.

Figure 10–6 Using the Profitunity Trading Partner.™

V. Making an Executive Decision
   A. Considerations
      1. Moving up one and/or two significant time frames to
         pinpoint current price action in the higher degree Elliott
         wave
      2. Going to a significantly lower time frame to pinpoint good
         trade location
   B. Execute
      1. Fractal
      2. Thumb signal
      3. Squat
   C. Flow =F - ocus
          L - et go
          O - bserve
          W - in!

Figure 10–6   (Continued)

SUMMARY

When you are operating at Level Three, you are in the top 3 percent of all traders in the world. You should be taking money out of the market on a regular basis and maximizing your ROI by your skill in allocating assets and varying the volume of contracts you are trading. Profitunity Planned Trading allows you to be minimally invested when the risk is greatest and maximally invested when the risk is least. If you can make profits trading on a one-contract basis, you should be able to double your percentage of ROI by varying the volume of contracts.

You need only one sheet of paper to record all your trading information. You have uncovered the underlying structure of the market and should be making it work for you. However a great deal more is at stake here than just making profits in the markets. The greatest leap in all of the five levels is the next step, from competent (Level Three) to proficient (Level Four). You will discover your own underlying structure and begin aligning it with the market's larger underlying structure.

You are now able to put into practice what you have learned about:

- How to read the individual bars;

- The current trend direction;

- The first indicators of a change in momentum;

- How to tell who is running the show;

- The meaning of increase and decrease in volume;

- How to measure the effect of incoming volume;

- How to trade the Profitunity windows;

- How to locate the current market in an Elliott wave;

- How to construct the 5/34/5 Profitunity MACD;

- How to identify and trade an initiating fractal;

- How to identify and trade a responsive fractal (thumb trade);

- How and when to place stops versus stop and reverses;

- How to use the Profitunity Trading Partner to simplify your analysis;

- How to always have an air bag in place and where to put it;

- How to determine and identify the market rhythm with the 5/13/34 moving average filter;

- How to use and monitor the 5/34/5 Profitunity MACD as the first change in momentum;

- How to trade through a five-wave Profitunity Planned Trading sequence.

To be a "great" trader requires not only monetary rewards but also enjoyment of the trading life. If you are addicted to the screen or spend 16 hours a day trading, you are not successful no matter how much money you take from the market. The still-missing link is found in the next two steps, Level Four and Level Five.

CHAPTER ADDENDUM

Let me share with you some vital research that has affected the world's Olympic teams since 1972 and will influence your trading and your life. Around 1952, several universities decided to study how to increase the effectiveness of various methods of improving athletic performance. Athletic performance was chosen because slight differences can be easily measured. For example, if a sprinter has been running the 100-meter dash for years, and, because of a training-method change, the sprinter's time improves even a fraction of a second, that change and its result become very significant. Similarly, if a competitive weight lifter is able to improve the maximum lift only a few pounds, that is significant.

These researchers were investigating the connection between motivation and results. They divided their sample population into two groups. The first group had a common psychological profile of doing an activity for the reward or payoff attached to that activity. For example, a high school freshman basketball player spent two hours after team practice each day shooting foul shots because the coach had said that, to make the varsity team, at least a 65 percent scoring average from the foul line was required. The payoff was: making the varsity team. Another hopeful was doing bench presses in the gym so that he would have a great chest and, when summer came, he would be more attractive to females on the beach. Payoff: attention from the females. An older man was a daily jogger because he feared a possible heart attack and had become convinced that jogging would increase his life span. Payoff: a longer life. The common characteristic in these examples from the first group was that the activity was being performed for the *deferred reward* or *later payoff.*

The second group, which was much smaller in number, differed from the first group in that they found the reward for each activity *inherent in the activity itself!* A freshman high school basketball player was staying after practice and shooting foul shots just because he liked to shoot foul shots. A weight lifter found his reward at the bench press in seeing whether he could press five pounds more than he had pressed the day before. An older jogger kept jogging because he enjoyed the endorphins that he felt after the first few blocks. The difference between these groups was vital, and the bottom line was astounding! The second group's improvement was not only four to six times as great but it occurred much faster! This study was replicated in dozens of universities with essentially the same results (Garfield, 1986).

In my own experience in working with thousands of traders, I have found that the greatest and most successful traders find their main reward in the activity of trading itself. Granted that most of us were originally attracted to trading by the idea of making a lot of money "without working for it," but I have found that the best and brightest get their kicks from actually *doing* the trading.

Nothing significant came from the universities' research, which was originally done in the early 1950s, until some athletics trainers from Bulgaria were visiting the United States and ran across the research. At that time, the East and the West were actively competing on all fronts—military, economic, and athletic. The Bulgarian trainers went back to the Eastern block countries with the American research in hand and completely changed their training methods.

This culminated in the East's sweeping the medals in the 1976 Summer Olympic Games in Montreal. Our defense, after being soundly beaten in almost every sport, was to accuse the Eastern block countries' athletes of using drugs. How else could they be the best in everything? However, drug tests on over 6,000 athletes turned up only two positives, and either or both could be attributed to ingestion of antihistamine tablets. The "secret" was that the East had trained the athletes so that their rewards and payoffs were inherent *in the activity itself* rather than being postponed for the day when they might win an Olympic medal.

The lesson here is: Do you really enjoy the act of trading? Or do you suffer from fear and greed every minute you are in the market? If you suffer, it is because you don't understand either the market and/or yourself. Most traders win or lose to the same degree that they understand themselves. Finding your own individual *underlying and unseen structure* is what Level Four and Level Five address.

World-class traders see the market itself as a support mechanism. Amateurs and/or less successful traders see the market as threatening. That difference is critical in achieving the last two levels and becoming an expert trader.

In Level Four, we will investigate the psychological side of trading. We will look at our own unique personal hardware, the neural wiring and interconnections in our brain, and our own personal choice of which software programs we want to run in our own brain.

REVIEW QUESTIONS

1. What is the importance of always looking for and using Profitunity Planned Trading (PPT)?

2. What are the advantages of using PPT trading techniques rather than just trading along with a comfortable volume of contracts and using fractal trading techniques?

3. What are the advantages of using the Profitunity Trading Partner worksheet?

4. What is the first column to fill in on the worksheet and why is it important to fill it in first?

5. What is the second column to fill in and why should it be second?

6. Why do you need to deal with two different time frames (the current one plus a significantly higher time frame) while trading?

7. What are the two or three primary trading signals?

8. Why shouldn't you just take these signals automatically and create a mechanical system for trading the market?

9. What factors are involved in making an executive decision about trading?

──11──

Level Four:
The Proficient Trader

The more I study physics, the more I am drawn to metaphysics.

Albert Einstein

GOAL: TO EXPLORE THE LINKS BETWEEN THE CHARACTERISTICS OF SUCCESSFUL TRADERS AND THE CHARACTERISTICS OF THE MARKET AND BETWEEN SELF-KNOWLEDGE AND PROFITABLE TRADING.

In this chapter, we make a radical departure from Levels One through Three. We now begin to work with our own underlying structure. If we can align our own underlying structure with that of the market, *winning becomes the path of least resistance.*

Using our earlier analogy, we identify pianists who reach this level as: those who begin to put a part of themselves into the music. A chord is sustained slightly longer; a crescendo is more gradual and controlled; a tempo is livelier. As listeners, we say these pianists have *feeling*. We noted earlier how the public forgives Frank Sinatra all his vocal inaccuracies and buys his records because he communicates feeling. The introduction of feeling is one of the important differences between Level

Three and Level Four. Feeling is something you don't get at the competent level in trading. Proficient traders feel a connection between themselves and the market; they no longer feel they are "outside" the market. They have become a part of a larger organism that we call the market. Their information, knowledge, and ideas seem to come out of nowhere. Their trading combines an effortless effort with "knowing without knowing how I know."

In this chapter, we will examine:

- How your body structure affects your trading style;

- How your brain is wired and is working while you are trading;

- Who the three different traders living in your body really are;

- How you and the market are alike.

Our study of chaos from economic, sociological, and personal psychological perspectives verifies our assumption that the market is really moved by millions of traders who are just like you and me and who are out there making risky decisions. The market can be thought of as a giant composite of these traders. An analogy might be the "stadium art" created successfully at events such as the Super Bowl and the Olympics, where each seatholder finds a color panel on his or her chair and, on signal, holds it as a contribution to a massive multicolored image. If we can understand ourselves, then we can understand the composite formed by the market. As we will see later in the chapter, the market is really a game of fantasy: sociological fantasy at the market level and psychological fantasy at the individual level.

A primary function of the market is communication—making public, on a real-time basis, what is happening in the pits.

The market beams the desires of traders around the world by posting the bid/ask prices and the times of those prices. As individual traders, we communicate (or cogitate) within ourselves while making our trading choices and then we communicate our decisions to the broker and ultimately to the floor.

PRINCIPLES OF HUMAN COMMUNICATION

When we envision the market as a composite of all the traders trading, we are acknowledging the market's important communication function. My training and experience in psychology have taught me that three principles of human communication that are true in the individual are also found in the market.

Principle 1: Ninety Percent of Everything We Hear Is Lies

What is going on in people's brain is not what comes out in their speech. Thoughts and feelings are modified by desires, fears, and anticipations. Suppose I am your employer and I ask you how you like working for my company. You actually hate both my company and me, but you need the income and have no idea where you might find another job. In this situation, you do not say, "Boss, I really hate your guts." You modify your wording into a response you think will be acceptable to me.

We disguise most of our communication, depending on present circumstances. We might look at someone of the opposite sex and say, "When I look into your eyes, time stands still." Paraphrased, the same message might be, "You have a face that would stop a clock," but the reaction to that statement would be quite different from the reaction to the first one. We constantly modify our communication to suit the immediate context and environment.

We also modify our communication by isolating various parts of our body and making them sites of behavior. We might say, "My head—*it* hurts" rather than the more accurate statement, "I am, for some reason, headaching myself." Or, "My throat—*it* is sore." Parallel statements in trading are subtle ways of not taking responsibility. For example, "My broker told me to go long, and I knew it was wrong." Or, "The stochastic—it said to buy and it was wrong again." These are typical ways of sidestepping responsibility and clarity.

Another way we cover up is by disguising our thoughts with words that seem to mean something else. Take the simple word *understand*. How often, when you use the word *understand* do you really mean *control*? Have you ever called a friend, a broker, or another trader, and commented, "I just don't *understand* this bond market, do you?" What you are really saying is, "I just don't *control* this bond market, do you?" Do you ever say to your kids, after some unacceptable behavior, "I just don't *understand* why you would do that." Again, you are really saying, "I just don't *control* you." Have you ever said to a spouse or friend, "You just don't *understand*." The real issue—and message—is *control*.

If you doubt the statement that 90 percent of all verbal communication is a lie, in the sense that it does not report accurately the thinking that is going on in the brain of the speaker, monitor yourself and others to see how truly honest you are in communicating your thoughts.

Principle 2: You Cannot Tell a Lie on All Channels

We are talking now about the whole person. We normally think we are communicating on two channels: (1) light waves and (2) sound waves (Figure 11–1). If I am in a room with you and you have reasonable sight and hearing, you can see what I am doing and you can hear what I am saying. Communication scientists have found that we actually communicate on five other channels plus two minor intraperson channels. The polygraph or lie detector is based on monitoring three of

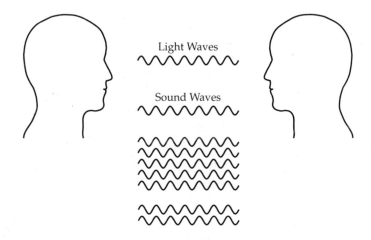

Figure 11–1 Person-to-person communication channels.

these nonverbal channels. The results are not admissible in court because the polygraph is fallible: it does not monitor all nine human communication channels. The best lie detector in the world is yourself when you listen without prejudice. Sometimes, this capacity is referred to as *intuition,* or even "women's intuition." If I tell you a lie verbally, I may have an eye twitch, a shoulder shrug, or a knee jerk; I may squirm, sweat, garble a sentence, or give some other physical signal that will indicate my lack of complete honesty.

Take an example that applies to males much more than females. When a man is listening to someone and he moves his hand to his jaw, scratches around the chin, or exhibits similar behavior—usually with his right hand if he is right-handed—that gesture means he believes what is being said or he is buying what is being sold, *at that moment.* If you are a broker attempting to sign up a new client by telling him the advantages of opening a commodity account, and he scratches his chin at the same time he is saying, "Well, I don't know if I really want to put that much money into commodities," your reply might well be, "Press hard; the third copy is yours."

Now let's take an example involving females. I am sure you have noticed that many females cross their legs while sitting down. Often, they will start swinging the crossed leg. This is usually a nonverbal way in which the female communicates her real feelings, which may or may not be spoken. Time is the crucial element here. If the female is swinging the crossed leg rapidly—about 60 times per minute or more—it communicates some sort of inner dissatisfaction. She may feel she is overdressed or underdressed for the occasion. She may just not feel well. She may not like the person she is with—or the person she is listening to.

If she has what research psychologists call "hip lateral mobility," which means she can move around as on a bar stool, the crossed foot will often point to the person or situation with which she is dissatisfied.

Interestingly, if the crossed leg is oscillating at much less than 60 times per minute, the female is expressing almost the opposite feelings. She is confident, she likes the people and the environment. Again, with "hip lateral mobility," she often points to whatever she finds satisfying.

We always tell the truth on some channel. Carl Jung once said, "If you want to understand human behavior, realize that we all have two tongues. One is in our shoe and the other is in our mouth and whether you understand [there is that word again] a person depends upon which one you listen to." In other words, what you do is more truthful than what you say.

Principle 3: People Can Only Talk about Themselves

If I say to you, "This room is a bit warm," I am not making a statement about the room. I am telling you about my nervous system. Even if I get very scientifically precise and say, "This room is exactly 21 degrees Centigrade," I am still telling you about myself and my approach to life. If I say, "That is a beautiful girl going by outside the window," I am not making a statement about the girl; I am talking about my standards of beauty.

The Human Communication Principles and the Market

The market follows these same principles of human communication because the market is not a separate entity. It is a composite of thousands of humans. Let's look at the principles in that perspective.

1. *Ninety percent of everything you hear about the market is lies* in that the messages do not reflect the truth of what is really going on. When you read the financial news or listen to CNBC-FNN, remember that the commentators get paid to talk, and talk they must. They have to say something about "why" the bonds went up, and at least 90 percent of what they say does not accurately portray what is happening in the market. They do not *know* what is happening, so how can they accurately describe it.

2. *The market itself cannot lie.* The bonds went up because they went up. There was more pressure to buy than to sell. To say it was "short covering" or a "technical bounce" is not the whole truth. We usually observe two channels in the market: (1) price and (2) volume that happens at a certain time. Just as in human communication, there are several more channels beyond price and time. In our fractal research, we use five channels.

3. *The market can only talk about itself,* and the language of the market is ticks. Ticks will always tell how the market feels. The conclusion here might be summed up as: "Listen to the music, not the words." The music is the real market and the words are commentary and/or opinion.

Our job at Level Four is to learn to listen at a much deeper level. To do that, we must understand ourselves at this deeper level.

HOW YOUR BODY STRUCTURE
AFFECTS YOUR TRADING

The largest cell in humans is the ovum, and the smallest cell in humans is the sperm. When the ovum permits the sperm to enter its outer wall and is fertilized, there is a cataclysmic explosion of energy. This energy is not evenly distributed. It concentrates more in one of three areas: (1) the endosperm (inside the center section), (2) the mesoderm (the area between the center and the outside), or (3) the ectoderm (inside but near the surface of the ovum). (See Figure 11–2.) Where this early energy concentrates at conception will determine what type of body the conceived child will have when it reaches adulthood.

An energy concentration in the center area results in a bulky (fatty tissue) round type of body. If the energy concentrates in the intermediate area (between the center and the outside), the body type is angular and muscular. If the energy concentrates around the outside (near the wall), a thin or slender body build results. These different body types carry the medical names of endomorph, mesomorph, and ectomorph,

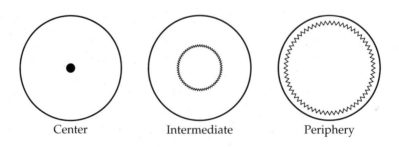

Center   Intermediate   Periphery

Figure 11–2   Possible energy concentration sites.

200

respectively. In actuality, we all have elements of each, but tend toward one of the three extremes. (See Figure 11–3.)

What we are discussing here is packaging. The most efficient package is a round ball. It contains the most "stuff" inside and has the least skin exposure outside. Human packaging determines and influences how people take in information. The ectomorph (thin person), with more skin exposure per pound of flesh than the other two types, is more sensitive to heat and cold. When persons with these three different body types look at a chart, they perceive and pay attention to different stimuli. The chart actually looks different to each type. Let's examine the body types in a little more detail and then apply our observations to trading.

In Figure 11–3, each type is classified with one word: the endomorph's word is *bulk*, the mesomorph's is *strength*, and the ectomorph's is *speed*. Because each has a different structural

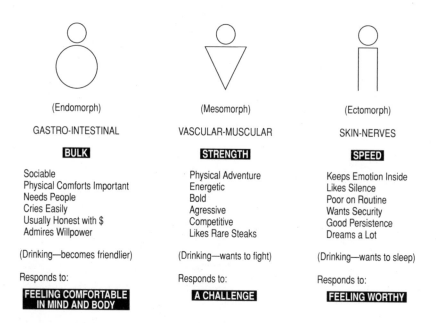

(Endomorph)	(Mesomorph)	(Ectomorph)
GASTRO-INTESTINAL	VASCULAR-MUSCULAR	SKIN-NERVES
BULK	**STRENGTH**	**SPEED**
Sociable	Physical Adventure	Keeps Emotion Inside
Physical Comforts Important	Energetic	Likes Silence
Needs People	Bold	Poor on Routine
Cries Easily	Agressive	Wants Security
Usually Honest with $	Competitive	Good Persistence
Admires Willpower	Likes Rare Steaks	Dreams a Lot
(Drinking—becomes friendlier)	(Drinking—wants to fight)	(Drinking—wants to sleep)
Responds to:	Responds to:	Responds to:
FEELING COMFORTABLE IN MIND AND BODY	**A CHALLENGE**	**FEELING WORTHY**

Figure 11–3   The three body types and their characteristics.

build, each becomes subject to unique irritations. For example, whenever endomorphs visit their doctor, odds are their problem is a gastrointestinal complaint. Mesomorphs' complaints to their doctor usually center around cardiovascular or muscular problems. When ectomorphs go to their doctor, their complaints center around skin or nerve problems. The packaging, or the relationship between their inner body and their skin, seems to hold a key.

It is not surprising that persons who fit the different body types crave and are motivated by different stimuli. Probably the predominant motivation to an endomorph is to feel comfortable. Think about people you know who fit this general category. Watch them while they move or sit. They tend to seek comfort and prefer easy ways of doing things, including trading.

Mesomorphs, however, are a different breed. They sometimes seem to be seeking "discomfort." They are outdoor "jock" types. What are they looking for and what makes them feel good? A challenge. Their attitude is, "Send me in, coach; I can do it." They constantly have to prove themselves and will then move on in search of other challenges. They are natural leaders and cheerleaders.

What the ectomorphs need most is to feel worthy. They want to do things that will prove they are capable, OK types of people. They are generally mediocre at performing repetitive, routine tasks, but they do very well in staff and project-type jobs.

None of these types is either good or bad, none is better than another. Body type is simply the hardware people are born with, and it is better to learn how to best use it than to be constantly frustrated.

There is one interesting example you can check for yourself. Go down on the trading floor and observe the body types of the traders. Over 95 percent of the locals have a mesomorphic build. One New York brokerage house attempts to hire only ex-hockey players to train as floor brokers.

Even chemicals and foods affect body types differently. Figure 11–3 indicates the reactions of each body type to alcoholic drinking. Endomorphs become friendlier. As their inhibitions fall, mesomorphs begin to seek more challenges, usually by raising their voices. Alcohol is a depressant rather than a stimulant to ectomorphs. They generally get drowsy, go to sleep, or leave the gathering early.

What does all this have to do with trading? A lot! Because your own body type will affect the way you take in information, you should trade within an environment that will assist and not hinder your effectiveness. A bulky, round trader should ensure comfort in every aspect possible. We recently worked with a very bulky, round trader who does quite well financially. He trades from a large, comfortable reclining chair in his living room. He has a 52-inch projection screen equipped with remote control. He uses the unit to watch the charts. He relaxes there during market hours, and trades via his portable phone.

Any of the three body types can be profitable in trading. It simply makes the job easier and takes away much of the strain if, as you trade, you take into account your natural body hardware. Know how you are packaged, and trade using the uniqueness and benefits of your personal body structure. Construct your trading environment to take advantage of your information processing techniques.

You also might consider getting regular deep-tissue body massage. It has been widely observed that when the body is limber and pliable, so is the mind. In trading, you need both a pliable body and a pliable mind.

In the next section, we will examine the neurological wiring of the human brain and how best to take advantage of the tremendous power contained in this personal twin-hemisphere necktop computer. It is important to remember that you will do your best trading when you utilize the uniqueness of your personal hardware.

Before we begin our study of the brain and how it contributes to trading success, an assessment is appropriate. So far, as we have covered Levels One, Two, and Three and their ancillary topics, we have covered how you *do trading*. We're about to deal with your being a trader. The market becomes part of you, and you become a part of the composite of people who are the market. This is the difference when you *are a trader*.

Knowledge, attitude, and commitment are key factors. When you purchase a major appliance, you receive special directions organized in an "Operating Instructions" booklet; when you buy a car, an owner's manual comes with it. But you have no owner's manual for your most important personal machinery, and that machinery is essential to the success of your trading. You define that success as: no more anxiety, anger, fear, jealousy, irritation, resentment, boredom, suffering, unhappiness, or lying to others about your results. This next section supplies you with a set of operating instructions so that you, your life, and your trading; your knowledge, attitude, and commitment; your brain and your brain programs can all be in more harmony. You're about to take advantage of the potential that has been locked in your head since before you were born.

THE HUMAN BRAIN

Nature vs. the Mapmaking of the Brain

First, humans do not have "a" brain; we have many brains. The right hemisphere, left hemisphere, and core are the main three brains.

In the left hemisphere (the part of your brain that is reading these words), $2 + 2 = 4$. In nature, this is not true at the universe level or at the level of quantum mechanics. The "laws" of arithmetic are true only because we voted to make them true and we now teach them as "the truth." Ask adults why $2 + 2 = 4$, and they will tell you, "Because it just does." Ask a second grader, and the truthful reply will be, "Because the teacher said so."

Our words and our concepts are an attempt to codify the world (chaos) to make it more understandable and more manipulatable. Often, truth is lost in this process. Another way to say this is: we are chronic mapmakers. Our feelings about the world and other people, and our thoughts about the world and the markets are all a process of abstraction or mapmaking. When we characterize today's market as being "choppy" or "trending," we are making a map to assist us in understanding the behavior of the market.

When I was first learning to pilot a plane, the instructors stressed that, while navigating and orienting a flight map to the territory below, it is crucially important to examine the territory first, then the map. If you are lost and you look for certain reference points on a map, you can almost always find some similar points on the ground. In aviation, this sequence could get you lost and cost you your life. In the market, it can cost you your fortune. *Never* look at the map until you have examined the territory (the market itself) first.

Much trading research has turned out to be disastrous as a result of looking at a map first. Market Profile, for example, was the darling of the trading world in the late 1980s. Thousands of traders thought it must be a godsend because it represented the market the way it "really is," making profitable trading easier. The effect has been just the opposite.

I, along with others, lost a great deal of money using this map. The problem is that Market Profile is based on parametric (linear) statistics—in particular, the concept of a normal distribution curve. Normal distribution and the concept of standard deviation simply do not adequately explain natural behavior or the markets. Literally, we get "lost" in the market.

In a linear world, cause and effect are very predictable: the effect can be predicted based on the force and direction of the cause. In a nonlinear world, this relationship between cause and effect does not exist. This is why fundamental, economic, mechanical, and technical systems do not make profits consistently in the market.

When we are not successful in predicting, the natural next step is to seek more information. In nonlinear systems, more information is often neither needed nor helpful. Complex behavior comes from simple iterations and nonlinear feedback.

The first step in learning how to use your brains for both better trading and better living is to realize that the way you have been "trying" to run your life and trading will always keep you bouncing like a yo-yo between temporary happiness (winning) and unhappiness (losing). This happens because you are working with the Type One underlying structure. You might want to reread the section on the structure of structure, in Chapter 4.

The Three Different Traders Living in Your Skin

Ever wonder why you often get so confused in trading? One prominent reason is that there are three different traders living in your body. Not just three different parts of your brain, but three *different personalities.* To make matters worse, they all have different goals and operating techniques, and they don't even speak the same language. Three distinctly different personalities are active, and only one of them is in charge at any moment. The trader-in-charge can change quite frequently, creating an enormous amount of inner confusion.

One trader is a consistent loser who always tries to buy the high and sell the low. One is an expert analyst but not a good trader. Another is a good trader but so-so at analysis. The final trader is in charge of intuition, inspiration, and insight. Each plays a different role in your trading.

A right–left split in the brain was first investigated in epileptic patients who had the dividing mechanism (corpus collosum) severed to reduce seizures. The researchers agreed that different parts of the brain seem to have different functions. For example, most people do math with their left hemisphere and perform music with their right hemisphere.

This popular conception is accurate, but it is not adequate. There are many splits and separations in the brain: left to right (more than one), back to front, top to bottom, and inside to outside. Here, we will limit ourselves to the three functional divisions: (1) the left hemisphere, (2) the core (including the spinal column and its connections), and (3) the right hemisphere. Each part of the brain seems designed specifically for certain types of thinking and behavior. Our purpose is to understand our necktop equipment in order to use it more effectively in trading.

There are really three different people living inside your head—not just three brains, but three very different personalities. They act differently and they see the world in entirely different perspectives. In fact, they don't even speak the same language. It is as though you live in a three-room apartment that you share with two other people. One of you lives in the living room and speaks Spanish, one lives in the kitchen and speaks Italian, and the other lives in the bedroom and speaks English. None of them is bilingual. In addition, each of you has very different skills and abilities. Each is completely dependent on the other two for survival. This can be a real problem if you don't cooperate.

Any one of you may trade, but only one is in charge at any moment. This internal division constitutes a major problem for extracting continuous profits from the market. To get the three internal traders working together, we must examine how they work and how they perceive both the market and the world. As we study each part, we will compare its power, purpose, and uniqueness to the whole and to the other parts, as they relate to trading behavior. We will look first at the left hemisphere.

The Left Hemisphere

You are using the left hemisphere of your brain, a.k.a. the conscious mind, to read this material. Of the three participants in your trading, this is actually the most "*un*-conscious." It is the only part of your brain that ever sleeps or goes unconscious.

The left hemisphere is the "idiot" of the trio we're studying. It is digital and sequential in design and can handle only about 16 bits of information per second. This limitation seems to be imposed by the speed limit at which neural impulses can travel in the nervous system itself. For example, when you are reading this page, light waves of varying intensity strike the retina of your eye and are converted into electrical impulses, which are then sent along the optic nerve to the back of the head. From there, after being sorted, they are sent to the association part of the brain, which is more toward the center of the head. The association part "re-creates" what we normally call writing (written or printed communications) and makes some type of interpretation based on factors already preprogrammed into the system from the core. It takes about 1/16 of a second for all of this to happen.

The time "lag" of 1/16 of a second means that we never see "right now." We are always looking at history at least 1/16 of a second later. The lag also makes it possible for us to "see" movies and television as continuous movement. What is really on the screen is a series of still pictures, flashing at the rate of 30 frames per second. Our left hemisphere cannot handle 21 individual images per second, so our brain merges them and they are communicated as movement. When movement is communicated with a flashing strobe light, jerky individual still pictures are projected. These are close to what your eyes really "see" all the time but at a higher number of frames per second. Movement is in the human brain, not on the TV or movie screen.

The left hemisphere is your Tasmanian Dragon, your despot, your gremlin, your no-good, sneaking, conniving saboteur that messes up your trading. Evolutionwise, this is the youngest member of your brain group. It is sometimes described as your "thinking mind" even though it is the idiot of your three boarders.

The biological purpose of the left hemisphere is to analyze and make *policy* and *judgment* decisions: what markets to trade, what type of money management to follow, how much time to spend in the market, and so on. It performs primarily a planning function, not a "carrying out" function. The left hemisphere makes the "what" type of decisions, not the "how" decisions. It is the *know what*, not the *know how* area. You could not ride a bicycle or even walk to the bathroom if you had only this brain. In trading terms, it is the left hemisphere's function to decide on perspective. It is not the left hemisphere's job to implement or find good trade locations.

The left hemisphere is characterized by a number of behaviors and abilities that exist only in this part of your neural system. Because it can handle only about 16 bits of information per second, you get confused if you are talking on the telephone and someone in the room starts to converse with you. Your circuit breakers blow and you lose your temper because you can't understand either of the people talking with you.

The worldview the left hemisphere gives you is one of struggle. If you were to cartoon it, it would be like climbing a never-ending set of stairs (Figure 11–4). This eternal struggle is suggested by a defect in our learning. We have been led to believe that climbing these stairs is not only unavoidable but is the only thing worth doing in this life. To the left hemisphere, this is a "dog-eat-dog world" and we had better do it to them before they do it to us.

Characteristics of a Left Hemisphere Trader

Five activities or characteristics that are important to traders occur only in the left hemisphere. Whenever you are aware of

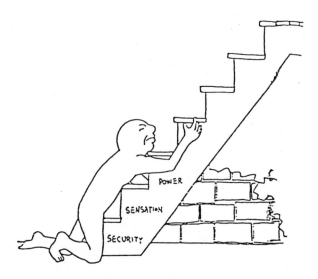

Figure 11–4 The stair-step worldview of the left hemisphere.

any of the behaviors described below, your left hemisphere is in charge at that moment.

1. *Language.* As you read this, your left hemisphere is running your show. No other part of you has the ability to read or speak the English (or any other) language. This part of you deals only with concepts; it does not deal directly with reality. All of your sensations come through the core, and the core controls your behavior. This is the primary reason that "positive thinking" does *not* work. The motto, "Every day in every way I am becoming a better and better trader" not only does not inspire but usually works in reverse because the core, which controls behavior, does not understand these words. Your sitting position as you read this, where your arms are, how the weight is going through your buttocks, the position of your legs, your respiration, heart rate, and so on, are all controlled "unconsciously" by the core.

210

Dreams come from your core, which is why you never dream that you are reading a book. Your core cannot read the English (or any other) language. The only exception is what is known as lucid dreaming, which is only experienced when you are not really asleep. If you could change your positive-thinking sentences into core (dream) language (moving, flying, emotional scenarios, and so on), you would have much better results.

2. *Time.* The sense of past, present, and future exists only in the left hemisphere. The core and the right hemisphere exist only in the ever-present *now*. You can only "get behind" or "hurry" from the left hemisphere. The core and the right hemisphere are never in a hurry. You don't hurry to grow your hair or digest your food.

3. *Judgment.* The sense of right and wrong, or better or worse, exists only in the left hemisphere. The core and the right hemisphere cannot imagine a "good" or a "bad" trade. That judgment is made only by the left hemisphere.

4. *No sense of humor.* The left hemisphere is like Dr. Spock in the *Star Trek* movies. Spock could reason deductively and inductively but could not have feelings or fun. Feelings come from the core and the right hemisphere.

5. *Effort or struggle.* Whenever you are struggling, the left hemisphere is in charge. That is the only part of you that can struggle. Any time you are talking or thinking in language, are aware of time limits, are trying to make a good trade, are not having fun and generally struggling, you are trapped in the left hemisphere. A more accurate description might be that you are *addicted* to the left hemisphere. As we will see later, this makes you the worst kind of trader. For example, if you feel the *necessity* to put on a *good* profitable trade and make a profit of $500 *before* the market closes today, you are doomed to failure.

Why? You are using the wrong maps, the wrong objective, the wrong tools, and the wrong part of your brain.

The philosophy of the left hemisphere is that you are responsible for your progress. There is no elevator or escalator. You must lift yourself up the never-ending stairway by your own bootstraps. This part of you is constantly comparing yourself and your progress to other traders: "Is their system or adviser better than mine? Should I be in the same markets they are in?" When we hear of another trader's success, we defend our egos by countering with, "Yes, but do you know how they blew out *last* year?"

If none of this helps our trading, how does the left hemisphere contribute to our success?

The Two Functions of the Left Hemisphere

Function 1: To "Habituate" Behavior

The biological design of the left hemisphere prepares it for two primary functions. The first function is to *habituate* behavior: it is a learning tool. Remember when you were first learning to ride a bicycle? You were asked to mount a two-wheeled piece of machinery that could not even stand up on its own and then sit on it as it moved down the street. You probably thought you could never master turning, balancing, pedaling, and braking to make the bicycle go where you wanted it to. Your left hemisphere had to handle all the details in the beginning. Slowly, as you gained both experience and confidence, the core started taking care of the details. Finally, you never thought anything about riding. You simply climbed aboard and went wherever you wanted to go.

To "habituate" behavior means to turn it over to the core and let the core attend to the details. The left hemisphere is simply not equipped to handle all the millions of details involved in even a simple behavior. For example, if you are sitting down, place your hand, palm down, on your thigh. Now raise your index finger about an inch. No problem, right? Do you realize that to perform that simple movement required the coordination of dozens of muscles, not counting the thousands of neural impulses required to initiate, direct, monitor, and stop that movement? If you had to get up to go to the bathroom right now and only your left hemisphere was functioning, you literally would die before you arrived there. Neither can you trade easily and profitably by depending on your left hemisphere.

One of our major goals is to habituate most of our trading behavior. If we trade with only the left hemisphere, we will commit financial suicide. As we gain experience beyond the competent level, we habituate more and more of our trading behavior. Experienced traders call this developing a "feel" for the market. That feel, like all our feelings, comes from the core. Athletes call this "the zone." Tim Gallway, in *The Inner Game of Tennis,* calls it "Self 2."

Function 2: To Solve Problems

The second primary function of the left hemisphere is to *solve problems.* Should I buy a car? Should I go long the bonds? Should I trade at all? Problem solving is an important and dynamic function for traders. However, it is also an important reason why traders do not make continuous progress in their skill in trading and in building up a capital base.

Let's take a common example that may have happened in your personal trading. Assume that one of the main reasons you want to be successful in trading is to solve the problem of your lack of money. Suppose you get lucky and/or good, and the money starts rolling in. The problem that drew you to the market is now being solved. What do you think is going on in your left hemisphere? "Hey, I am working myself out of a job. What if I am not needed around here any more?" The left hemisphere, being a true bureaucrat, can't take that chance. So it does the only thing it can do: it creates more problems! How? Usually, by making dumb decisions that set up losing trades. Later in this section, we will develop a Profitunity technique that will eliminate this fear in the left hemisphere.

This tendency, so common in trading, pervades all of life. A general principle of human behavior is that as soon as we start to become successful, we tend to stop doing the very thing that made us successful in the first place. During a courtship, we are on our best behavior. We are thoughtful and considerate; we pay attention. As soon as the marriage is under way, we start paying attention to more pressing, more important information. We start taking our partner for granted. After a period of time, we may start wondering what happened. Similarly, as soon as we start to become successful in trading, we start taking the left hemisphere for granted. It comes back on us with a vengeance, bringing new and bigger problems to solve. It does not wish to lose its job of solving problems.

The script that most traders follow is: struggle, make a few good winning trades, and end up giving it all (and maybe a bit more) back to the market. The normal outlet is to blame the perversity of the market for not winning consistently. However, the real blame almost always belongs closer to home, inside the left hemisphere. This no-good gremlin is out for its own hide, not the good of the organism—you. Later, we will examine a number of ways to tame and train your gremlin like left hemisphere.

One of the most profitable insights in trading is a realization that continuous good trading is much more a process of "letting go" of ideas that don't work than one of doing more. When riding a bicycle, you don't constantly ask for other bikers' opinions, and you forget the struggle you had years ago when you thought you would never learn to ride a two-wheeler. Let's examine now this much smarter part of you—your core.

THE CORE

Physically, the core consists of the limbus, the reticular activating system, the thalamus, the hypothalamus, and the whole spinal section of the brain. The left hemisphere is analogous to a digital computer; the core is more like an analog computer. Our survey of research indicates that the core can handle from 500,000 to 3,000,000 bits of information per second, compared to the left hemisphere's measly 16 bits per second. If you were to close your eyes right now and name every item you remember seeing in the room where you are sitting as you read this, you might be able to list 30 to 75 items. However, if you were hypnotized (hypnotism gives access to the core), you most likely could list several hundred or even thousands of items.

You are only aware of seeing a portion of what the retina sends down the optic nerve. Think, can you hear birds? A clock ticking? An air conditioner? Automobiles or maybe a plane outside? Where were they before you thought about them? The core knew they were there. Most information must be filtered out by the reticular activating system because the left hemisphere can handle only a measly amount of input compared to the core or right hemisphere. That is why we see stupid errors in trading after the fact rather than in the present tense.

The core needs this power because it basically handles our entire life. It decides about our blood temperature, the carbon dioxide level in the blood, whether we need another drop of hydrochloric acid to finish digesting that last bit of food in the stomach. It tells us when we are sleepy, hungry, thirsty, and so on. If there were some possible techniques to harness all this power for trading, would it help? You bet it would. And therein lies the big difference between the ordinary successful trader and the outstanding leader in trading. Level Four trading brings the core into our trading activities.

Recall that one of the main functions of the left hemisphere is to habituate behavior—to "teach" the core to take over the various operations that the left hemisphere has neither the time nor the power to coordinate.

The core controls your behavior when you aren't consciously focused on it. All your five senses must go through the core before you can become conscious of them. In hypnosis, the left hemisphere is temporarily sidelined, and suggestions go directly to the core. When that happens, behavior changes dramatically. In firewalking workshops, hours are spent "getting the student ready" in both body and mind. Suggestions of confidence are given over and over until the left hemisphere habituates that feeling by allaying the fear and allowing the core to take over. Because the core does not understand spoken language, visualization is used extensively. The negative left-hemisphere words "don't burn" are abandoned; instead, the image of "cool moss" is created in the core. The only people who get burned in a firewalking seminar are those who are unsuccessful in transferring responsibility to the core.

Have you ever been driving down a highway and suddenly realized that you don't remember driving through the last town? If *you* don't remember, who was driving? The core, of course. Or have you ever had the experience of narrowly missing a serious car wreck? After the scare was over and you replayed the incident, you realized that you automatically did whatever was necessary to save you from being seriously hurt. The core was working again. The core is a genius compared to the left hemisphere. Yet, almost everything the core knows behaviorally was taught to it by the idiot left hemisphere. If your left hemisphere taught the core some behavior that is not as successful as you wish, you can reteach it.

When you are operating from your core, life seems like a roller coaster ride (Figure 11–5). Let's examine the differences in outlook between a stair-step type of world and a roller coaster world. On the roller coaster, it is not nearly as important where you are in the progression of the ride. Even if you

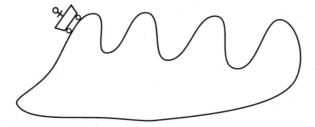

Figure 11–5   The core as a roller coaster ride.

are at the highest pinnacle of the ride, you know what is coming next—a stomach-wrenching drop toward the ground. That
is not too depressing because you know you will soon be at the
top again.

Time, for the core, resembles a circle rather than a straight
line. In fact, the core is not concerned with the "progression of
time." Things and events simply are either "now" or "not
now."

The core is the originator of all your feelings. What happens physiologically is that the core determines what to do
with the "juices" of the body—the blood, interstitial tissue
fluid, other body liquids. Because the body is mostly liquid, it
is a very pliable piece of machinery. When you get fearful, the
core directs the juices of the body to the abdominal region. It
does this for a good reason: protection. When you are angry or
have rage, the juices flow quickly to the muscle tissue, enabling
you to take action. You probably can't keep still when you're
very angry. Your juices are stimulating the muscles to move,
often dramatically. When you are very happy, in love, romantic, feeling really good, the juices flow to the skin. That's why a
young couple, newly in love, seems to just gleam. Many pregnant mothers glow because they are happy and the juices are
moving to the skin. Every feeling you have is caused by variation of this "juice flow."

What does all this have to do with trading? Everything! If we can get in touch with our core, we can control our juices, our feelings, our sensations, and our trading.

Now we come to a problem that you probably have already anticipated. If the core is so powerful and if everything that we think about in the left hemisphere comes from the core, there has to be a gigantic "file cabinet" and/or "trash can" between the core and the left hemisphere. Something, somewhere has to decide which 16 bits of information, from the average 3,000,000 coming in each second, to send to the left hemisphere. Physiologically and probably psychologically, that transmitter is the reticular activating system (RAS).

The RAS, located between your ears, is one of the best protected areas of your entire body (Figure 11–6). It is about the size of your little finger, and 70 percent of all your brain cells have a connection to it. If you damage it in any way, you fall into a coma and remain in a coma until it starts working again. When you go to sleep tonight, your RAS has sent a message to your hypothalamus to secrete a bit of a hormone known as

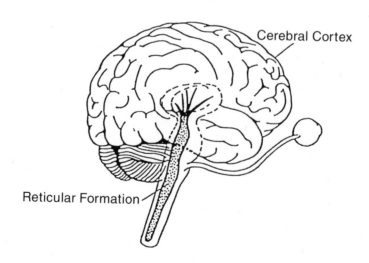

Figure 11–6 The reticular activating system.

serotonin, which lets the left hemisphere retire for a while. (Remember that the left hemisphere, our so-called conscious mind, is the only part of your body that goes unconscious or sleeps.) One of the primary functions of the RAS is to determine or decide what information is sent to your left hemisphere (conscious mind).

Because this function of "paying attention to" is so important and vital to successful trading, we must ask: How does the RAS learn to decide? It is almost a paradox that the left hemisphere, which is totally dependent on the RAS for an information filter, also teaches the RAS what it should pay attention to. This teaching happens through the habituation process, which we discussed earlier. Let's look at a couple of examples. When you walk down a busy city sidewalk, you hear hundreds of footsteps and you pay absolutely no attention to them. When you are at home and a member of the family walks down your wood-floor hall, you recognize who it is by the footsteps. But when you are awakened in the middle of the night and think you hear strange footsteps, your entire body/mind goes on alert. Very different reactions are triggered by whether the RAS permitted the information to reach the left hemisphere. This process is almost totally automatic: you are not consciously aware of it from the left hemisphere.

In trading, what you notice when the market moves is what you have taught your RAS to notice through past experience and your left-hemisphere evaluation of that past experience. This brings up one of the vital keys to successful trading: *simply noticing.* This activity is unbelievably difficult for most of us. We believe we are constantly doing it when in reality we almost never do it. Let's do an experiment here. Your participation consists of simply observing, *without changing anything,* an activity that you have done hundreds of times already today with no difficulty. Let me tell you beforehand: this is a tough thing to do. I want you to observe your breathing pattern.

219

Most participants have one of two reactions: they either start breathing a little deeper or they hold their breath. Did you make any small change in your breathing? If so, you are not simply observing. Probably the judgmental function of your left hemisphere came in and said, "What am I supposed to be doing?" or "Should I breathe a bit deeper?"

Let's try an even more illuminating experiment. This time, as you simply observe, I want you to do something else that you have done hundreds of times already today—something so vital that you could live only a short time without doing it. It's easy. You know exactly and precisely how to do it, and you do it so often you don't even notice doing it 99 percent of the time. In fact, you were doing it even before you were born.

Your task is to swallow five times as fast as you can (without drinking or eating anything) and notice how you do it.

Did you do it? If not, please don't read any further until you do. It is very important.

What changes did you notice in your ability to swallow, each time you attempted to do it on purpose? It not only became more difficult but it took longer to accomplish it each time, right? Why? Because you were trying to do a job that had long ago been habituated to your core. When you focus the spotlight of the left hemisphere on swallowing, it interferes with the vital functions of that powerful core. This is exactly what happens while trading. Most trading should be a function of the core. When we focus left-hemisphere attention on it, it becomes unbelievably difficult and less profitable. Analysis of the market is a left-hemisphere function; the act of trading is a core and right-hemisphere function.

The uniqueness of your core brain is the amount of information it can handle and sort out. When it is used appropriately, you have no feelings of hurry, judgment, use of language, or struggle. You are also having good feelings and a good time.

THE RIGHT HEMISPHERE

We know that the core is literally hundreds of thousands of times more powerful than our "conscious" left hemisphere, but no one seems to know the exact power of the right hemisphere. As for its function, the right hemisphere is the source for the three big "I's":

Inspiration

Insight

Intuition

When your right hemisphere is running the show, every-thing seems effortless. Instead of a struggle created by the left hemisphere or a roller coaster created by the core, the right hemisphere is just a "float down the river" (Figure 11–7). Life (the market) itself is a support mechanism. You seemingly can do no wrong. You need a downtown parking space and one magically opens up. Everything in life seems to be geared for

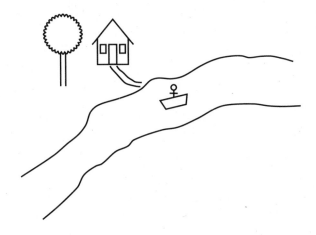

Figure 11–7   The world of the right hemisphere.

your personal happiness. It is the absolute opposite of the left hemisphere dog-eat-dog world.

Putting the three brains into computer language, we would say that the left hemisphere is the programmer and the software, the core is the central processing unit (CPU), and the right hemisphere is a universal modem connecting this CPU to all the other CPUs in the universe.

The right hemisphere is the least known and least understood component of the nervous system. We cannot even begin to evaluate the power that this hemisphere contains. Its power seems almost infinite.

Its uniqueness lies not only in its power but also in its seemingly unlimited capacity for knowledge. Maybe this is what Galileo meant when he said, 300 years ago, "You cannot teach anyone anything, all you can do is to reveal to them what is already inside of them." Some religions address this part of a person. Christianity teaches that "the kingdom of heaven is within." Buddha said, "If a person cannot turn to himself, who can he turn to?"

In holographic terms, the right hemisphere may contain the knowledge and the blueprint of the universe. If this supposition is anywhere near accurate, we certainly want to access this source in our trading. How do we access it? By getting out of our limiting left hemisphere, which means going beyond language, forgetting time, giving up trying, quitting judging, and having a good time. Is this transition the reason trading is so rewarding and so frustratingly difficult at the same time?

Figure 11–8 shows various balances among the different minds and how their combination will affect trading. For example, traders who are dominant and trade primarily from their left hemisphere will lose because they are scared and they do the wrong things at the wrong time. Those who trade only from the core will lose because of recklessness. Those who trade only from the right hemisphere will lose because of bad management.

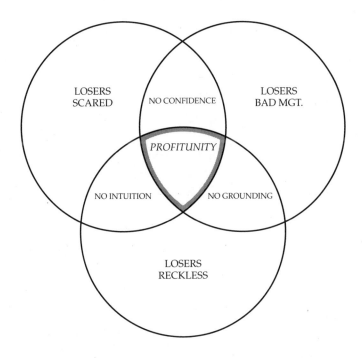

Figure 11–8   Three-brain model with overlaps.

If one trades with both left hemisphere and core but not enough right hemisphere, that trader will lack intuition, insight, and inspiration. If one trades with too little left hemisphere, that trader will have a lack of grounding. If one trades with too little of the core involved, that trader will experience a lack of confidence. What becomes obvious from the model is that the most efficient and profitable way to trade is to use all three brains and make the trading completely "mindful." We are searching for a better understanding of how we mix these three minds in our trading recipe. In Level Five, we will examine the four possible "software" programs our minds use when we trade.

One of the most interesting characteristics of your intrapersonal inhabitants is that you can always tell in an instant which one is in command. The way the world looks to you at this moment will tell you exactly which one is in charge. If your life at this instant is a struggle, you are concerned about time and language, you dearly want to do the right thing, and/or you aren't having fun, your left hemisphere is definitely in charge. If, on the other hand, life is a series of ups and downs, you feel good physically, and you are having a good time, you are operating from your core. If life is absolutely a bowl of cherries and everything in the world seems to be geared to giving you exactly what you want, you are in the right hemisphere.

SUMMARY

At Level Four, we step outside the boundaries of classical physics and the Aristotelian world. The science of chaos has given us insights into the natural workings of both the market and ourselves. We now understand that we are a microcosm of the market: we have very similar characteristics and behaviors. This gives us better insight into how to deal with the market and, more importantly, our own personal behavior within the market itself.

We now know that most traders lose because they do not use their brains the way they were biologically designed to be used. They have the tools; they just pick the wrong ones for the job of trading.

We also know that our greatest enemy in trading is not the market, programmed trading, big pools, or floor traders. Our greatest enemy is misusing our own left hemisphere. When we use the left hemisphere to trade, it always creates fear and does the wrong thing at the right time. The function that creates the most difficulty is the left hemisphere's own internal function of solving problems. It creates a "back-and-forth" structure. Winning creates losing, because one of the left hemisphere's functions is to solve problems. If there are no problems, then the left hemisphere must create some, to have continuous employment.

The greatest fear of the left hemisphere is to not survive. If there are no problems to solve and the left hemisphere cannot create some, it may be "laid off." The key here is to work from a different substructure where there is a completely different attitude about not having problems to solve.

We know that the power of the right hemisphere may approach infinity. Nothing in our educational system concentrates on or develops this most powerful part of our equipment. It develops naturally when we "let go" as we habituate our left hemisphere learning.

At this level of trading, continued improvement in results is 99 percent letting go and only 1 percent learning more.

Mozart, the most spectacular composer of all time, said that his music always came to him in an instant. He did not hear it from start to finish, it all happened in a heartbeat. In the right hemisphere, time and space are flexible.

It is interesting to note that modern physics, with its billions of dollars and its human resources for pushing the edge of research, is coming to the same conclusions that ancient meditators arrived at through an inner examination of their own thoughts and minds.

Assuming that all of this is true, how do we incorporate it into our lives and our trading? We examine that question in the next chapter, as we see what makes an expert and how an expert thinks and trades.

REVIEW QUESTIONS

1. What are the three principles of communication that apply both to individuals and to the markets?

2. What do you feel is your own predominant body structure?

3. What one word would sum up your predominant characteristic?

4. Based on question 3, how could you set up your trading to be most effective and what are you looking for?

5. What are the three different traders living in your skin?

6. Name the five behaviors that occur only in the left hemisphere.

7. What are the two functions of the left hemisphere?

8. What part does the left hemisphere play in your trading?

9. Why do you lose when you trade from the left hemisphere?

10. How much stronger is the core than the left hemisphere?

11. What sorts of activity does the core control?

12. How powerful is the right hemisphere?

13. In remembering the purpose of the right hemisphere, what do the three I's represent?

12

Level Five:
The Expert Trader

Since nobody is quite sure why we were put on this earth in the first place, I suppose we might as well have as good a time as we can.

Herb Caen
Column, October 6, 1992

GOAL: **TO UNDERSTAND THE PERSONAL BELIEF SYSTEMS AND PERSONAL TRADING PROGRAMS WE CARRY WITH US TO THE MARKET AND TO LEARN HOW TO INTEGRATE THEM WITH THE UNDERLYING STRUCTURE OF THE MARKET**

You are now approaching the pinnacle of trading, where almost everything you do increases your growth, satisfaction, profit, and happiness. You have traveled a road experienced by very few ordinary citizens and less than 1 percent of all traders. You have examined and now understand the underlying structure of the market. That knowledge enables you to become consistently profitable. You have analyzed your own underlying and usually unseen structure. By aligning your own underlying structure with that of the market, you can make consistent winning *the path of least resistance.*

In this chapter, you are trading your own states of mind. This Olympic level of trading shares many characteristics with champions in any endeavor, including sports. Remember how Michael Jordan would take a foul shot? He would look first at the basket, then down at the floor while he bounced the basketball three times. Why always three times and never four or two? That was his way of letting go of his left hemisphere and having his core and right hemisphere take over. He had learned years before how to make a foul shot. His job at the four line was to *not* get in his own way.

In trading, as in sports, your brain is not always your friend. If you are on the 18th hole in a golf tournament and need to make an eight-foot putt to win, is your brain your friend? No. It almost always gets in your way. That's why Jack Nicklaus always does four dry putts. He knows how to putt, and he is not aiming at the hole. His job at this point is to get his left hemisphere out of the way.

Michael Jordan and Jack Nicklaus spent years learning to make, respectively, a perfect foul shot and a perfect putt. Their job is to deliver *now,* and they can do that best by getting the idiot brain out of the way and letting the more intelligent brain do the job it was biologically designed to do.

To examine this at a deeper level, we must go inside our unconscious belief systems. They become our paradigms or the lenses through which we view the world. To examine our own personal worldviews, we must look at reality and our concept of reality.

BELIEF SYSTEMS AND REALITY

Let's start with a base that is as generic as possible. Let's describe reality as: what *is* at this moment. What *is* is that you are reading this paragraph. For our discussion, everything else is nonreality, at least to us at this moment. For generic purposes, let's call this what-is-right-now reality *space 1*. Everything else, we will label *space 2*. (See Figure 12–1.)

Space 1 is what is, or reality; space 2 is what isn't, or nonreality or fantasy. An important part of our culture is that few of us are interested in reality. Reality is usually too boring to be motivating. We become more motivated by fantasy. You are reading this book because you have a fantasy that by reading it you will learn what you need to improve your results in trading and thereby be happier. Our mutual hope is that your fantasy will become reality, if it hasn't already.

Pepsi reportedly paid Michael Jackson over $28 million to make a few short TV commercials. Pepsi is a pretty smart company and wouldn't be paying anyone $28 million for a few minutes of videotaped commercials unless there was a solid probability that it would pay off. Pepsi knows how people think and how fantasies motivate buyers.

Millions of people have watched these commercials, in which Jackson is dancing. What goes on unconsciously in viewers' minds is: "If I drink a Pepsi, I could dance like Jackson." That far-flung fantasy still sells billions of Pepsis.

Our lives seem too occupied with making up fantasies and then attempting to make them come true. Our fantasy of having more money runs our lives. We have a fantasy that if we buy bonds on the opening tomorrow, we may make some real profits. We tend to forget we are buying from someone who has just as strong a fantasy that the bonds are going down. Sometimes a fantasy is wrong; but you already knew that.

SPACE 1   SPACE 2

What *is*   What *isn't*
Reality   Nonreality
     Fantasy

Figure 12–1   Space 1 and space 2.

One way to diagram life is as a constant effort to make our fantasies come true. We make up ideas, put them in space 2, and try to actualize them into space 1.

We now come to a crucial distinction: How do we make space 2 into space 1? Success in achieving our fantasies is dependent on the underlying structure of space 1, space 2, and the space between them. Let's make some statements about life and then apply them to trading.

Understand first that I probably don't have a thimbleful of missionary blood in my body. I am not trying to convince you of anything. Look at these concepts and if they help you, use them; if not, don't use them. They have been vital to the success of hundreds of real-time traders. The vocabulary I use is important here, and I have emphasized the key words. Each statement is followed by a short commentary.

1. Life is a **GAME** in which **WE MAKE WHAT ISN'T** more important than **WHAT IS.**

I mean the word **GAME** in its biggest and most important sense. It is not denigrating in any respect. The words **WE MAKE** indicate this is our choice. Not all cultures in the world make up fantasies the way we do. **WHAT ISN'T** refers to our fantasy, and **WHAT IS** refers to the current reality.

2. The most important reason to play this **GAME** is to **FIND OUT WHO WE ARE.**

For most traders, this game of trading is a very psychological primordial event. Our ego, our bragging rights, and usually our self-worth are all on the line. If our primary purpose for trading is to make a bunch of money and we lose, our ego suffers and our perspective is usually upset. The most important commodity you will ever manage is *your own perspective.* Above all else, it should be nurtured and protected. If your perspective is upset, you will try to "double up and catch up," do the "big one," and usually get creamed.

However, if your most important reason for trading is to find out who you are, another scenario will unfold. On a losing day, you can sit back and say, "Gee, isn't it interesting how I react to losing $_____ today." It may be tough, but you still have your perspective intact and can come back and try again without your tools (brains) being distorted.

The primary reason for doing anything is to find out who you are. This book is intended to help you toward that personal knowledge.

3. The only way to play this game in such a way that you find out who you are is to realize that **WHAT WAS**—before you made **WHAT ISN'T** into **WHAT IS**—was totally **OK.**

By following this last statement, you ensure that you are using the Type Two structure that we discussed in Chapter 4. The key difference is that, in a Type One structure, you are making up your fantasy to solve a problem in space 1. In that sense, you are denying the current reality. In a Type Two structure, you are accepting the current reality and *allowing* that current reality to expand until it encompasses space 2. Let's walk through an example.

Oprah Winfrey is/was a fat lady. I am going out on a limb and attributing to her things that I don't really know; however, after dealing with thousands of patients in psychotherapy and growth situations, I do believe what I am saying is accurate. Oprah's space 1 was a fat lady and her space 2 (fantasy) was to be a skinny lady. Several years ago, she went on a diet and became skinny enough to make commercials for Guess jeans. A bit later, she ballooned up beyond her original weight. The crucial question: Why didn't she stay skinny? Because she was using the wrong underlying structure to make the journey from space 1 (what is) to space 2 (what isn't).

For whatever reasons, she did not want to be a fat lady. Maybe she thought that being skinny would create more viewers for her TV show, or that she would have a better love life. The specific content of her desires is unimportant; the critical item is *why* was she making up the fantasy. If it was to "get rid of a problem" in space 1, the current reality, it sets up the back-and-forth pendulum model described in the structure of structure in Chapter 4.

To get into a Type Two structure of structure, the current reality must be totally OK. Before Oprah can really become a skinny lady inside and outside and have no problem staying skinny, it must be OK for her to be a fat lady. The question immediately becomes: If it is OK to be a fat lady, why change? There is the paradox. Because there is no reason for change, there is also no reason *not* to change. We have arrived at *choice.*

Putting this into traders' terms, until it is totally OK for you to be a loser, you most likely will never be a consistent, easy trading winner. You hear this fact restated in several different ways: "Scared money never wins," "Love your losses," and other proverbs. They never meant much to me until I understood the Type Two underlying structure. Being freely at choice is probably one of the best advantages you could acquire as a trader.

Here is the vital key. Whenever you are making up your fantasy in space 2, the most vital question you can ask is: Why am I creating this fantasy? If it is to solve a problem you are having in space 1, it will not work on any permanent, easy basis. It will set up a figure-eight pathway where solving a problem immediately creates another problem to bring you back where you started.

As represented in Figure 12–2, a pendulum, propelled by momentum, swings through dead center. As it leaves dead center, the momentum starts dying out as gravity becomes a greater and greater force. Finally, gravity takes over, and the pendulum reverses and starts moving in the opposite direction. Then momentum leads to gravity, which leads to momentum, which leads to gravity, and so on.

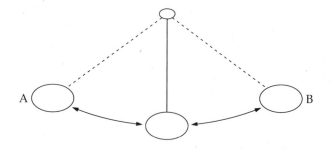

Figure 12–2   The pendulum and type one structure.

In the market, this behavior is often displayed by traders who decide they cannot afford a large loss. They set their stops tight. Their trade is triggered, and the market backtracks just enough to get them out of the market, then zooms off in the direction they thought it would go when they placed the trade in the first place. The traders decide, "The problem is that the stops are too close. The market needs room." On the next trade, they set the stop far back, to give the market room. The trade is triggered and the market starts backtracking all the way to the distant stop. Disgusted and disappointed, they think to themselves, "I can't take that kind of loss. I must tighten my stops again." This is probably the most common trading example I can give you of Type One structure. Whatever behavior you are exhibiting turns into the opposite behavior. The only constants are continual change in strategy and consistent losses.

Anyone on a yo-yo diet, anyone who quits smoking and still desires a cigarette, anyone who quits drugs and still desires them, and anyone who quits drinking and still wants a drink are trapped in this back-and-forth structure.

The main reason so many of us are stuck in the Type One structure is fully discussed in Chapter 4, where we examined our Aristotelian heritage as opposed to the Heraclitan heritage. Remember that the Heraclitan philosophical approach has given us the theory of relativity, quantum mechanics, and the science of chaos. To further emphasize this difference and its effects, go with me now on a *Reader's Digest* type of condensation of what you would most likely learn if you spent some time in graduate school studying psychology.

Psychology and Belief Systems

The first thing you must know is that the first psychologists were disenchanted priests who were already doing religious counseling and decided it would be more rewarding to do that in the secular world. They looked around for models on which to base their new programs. At that particular time in history (it's not that different now), science and medicine were the big kahunas—science because the scientific approach using controlled experiments was the growing rage, and medicine because it used the scientific method and could get reliable controlled results.

Through the years, the similarities have been astounding. First-year medical students take a course called gross anatomy and are assigned to dissect a cadaver. This lab is usually either in the basement of the Medical School building or, more commonly, in the basement of the teaching hospital. All first-year graduate students in psychology take a course called animal behavior, and it is almost always conducted in the basement of the psychology building.

In this psychology course, students are first told that their subjects for study are white rats because of the similarity between the neurological system of a rat and that of a human. Dozens of animals are much closer to humans neurologically than rats, but rats are cheap!

Students collect their school-issued white lab coats, which make them God in the land of rats. They are then given their little rat and their task: Motivate the rat, then educate him, and finally frustrate him. The purpose: to learn about how animals and, by inference, humans behave.

Motivating the rat is simple: starve him. No food for a day or so, and he is motivated. Next, he is placed in a maze with some good-smelling cheese at the end of one of the maze tunnels. The rat is not stupid. He smells the cheese and takes off wildly down the various corridors. He pauses only long enough to try to determine where the tunnel is that holds that delicious and needed cheese.

After a spell of rather frantic rambling, the rat finds the cheese, gobbles it up, and returns to being an unmotivated rat. (Hunger was his motivation and he temporarily cured that problem.) Remotivation begins: he is placed back in solitary confinement for another three days or so.

The same process is repeated over and over. To educate the rat, the cheese is placed at the end of the same tunnel in each repetition of the experiment. The students must educate their rat before midterm, or else.

The rat soon learns that the cheese is at the end of the same tunnel every time he enters the maze. Before too long, he quits wandering up and down the halls of the maze and goes directly to where the cheese is. Once he has done that a required number of times, he is indeed an educated rat. By definition, an educated rat is a rat "who knows where the cheese is."

The students' next job is to frustrate the rat and examine his reactions closely. If the students can learn to handle a frustrated rat, they someday may be able to handle a frustrated human. Who knows, they may even be able to handle their own frustrations.

They let their hungry friend out, and he rushes to the tunnel where the cheese has always been. His education is demonstrated by the fact that he engages in no exploratory behavior. He *knows* where that cheese is. It has always been there and it should be there now. But it isn't.

(A trader, at this point in a comparable sequence, might say, "It is the end of the fourth wave and it should go up, but it isn't.")

The students look very carefully at this little guy's face when he discovers that the cheese isn't where it isn't where it is supposed to be. His expression conveys that he is thinking, "I must have counted wrong." Every time the students educate a rat and then frustrate him, he starts repeating what he has always done. He goes all the way back to his starting gate in the maze and starts counting again.

But there is no cheese there now. After a brain-numbing number of tries, the exhausted rat, who by this time is dragging his tired nails over the floor of the maze, finally wanders down the hall and tries out another tunnel.

What can we learn from this exercise? This laboratory rat is a lot smarter than most humans. The rat will finally give up and get something that works better for him. Most humans will live and die in a "tunnel" where there is no cheese. A common definition of insanity is: doing the same thing over and over and expecting different results.

If you are living in a tunnel, which may be your world and/or your trading, how do you make peace with yourself if you're not getting the cheese? How do you then spend your life? If you are a scientist, you may spend your life studying two square inches of the tunnel wall. You may learn everything it is made of and get recognized for that knowledge. You may even receive a Nobel prize for knowing more about the tunnel wall than anyone in the world. But you are still in the tunnel.

If you are attracted to studying human behavior, you may become a counselor, psychologist, or psychiatrist. You are then taught that your main job is to make people's deviant behavior more "adaptable." I had a professor in graduate school who opened the class every Friday morning with, "Remember, guys, hams are cured, not people!" and laugh knowingly every time. Actually, we psychologists are in one of the few professions where the worse the job we do, the more we get paid. If it takes me three years to "cure" you, I get paid more than a better colleague who can do it in three months. I have often heard therapists at conventions talk about their ability to "hold" patients.

We must make peace with the tunnel we live in, when it does not contain enough nourishing substance—food, love, or profits. This tunnel is really our state of mind which was built by the person we see every day in our mirror. We all built our own individual tunnels. Are we really proud of them?

At Level Five, we are at the point of being able to choose our own tunnel. If we don't like it, we can build another bigger, better tunnel that is a lot more fun to live in. That is what this chapter is about: trading our states of mind.

In Chapter 11, you learned how to tell which of your three brain personalities is running your show at the moment. Nature has a beautiful way of balancing out all equations. In return for external effects' letting us see ourselves, we constantly tell the world which of our own software programs we are running at that moment. We are always running one of four different programs; our necktop computer can run only one at a time. However, we can switch them quickly enough to give an impression that more than one is running simultaneously.

If we choose to align our states of mind with the composite state of mind of the market, we need a different type of indicator. In the early 1980s, I realized that no indicator on the market really gave me what I needed to trade successfully. My conclusion, at that time and even more so now, was that no one trades the market; we all trade our own individual belief systems. But there was no way to measure the composite of belief systems of all the traders currently in the market. I was only interested in *active* traders. No matter what someone's belief system is, it has no effect on the market if that person isn't participating in the trading process.

In an effort to bridge this gap (a lack of indicators) and to further our understanding of the market in general, we started a research project to determine what percentage of traders were running each of the four basic psychological programs in trading. We recorded the percentages and then, a year later, repeated our study with almost identical results. The following section gives our findings and explains how they can be used to further your own trading success.

YOUR PERSONAL TRADING SOFTWARE PROGRAMS

In your personal trading software "file," you have four different programs or "disks":

1. Self-preservation program;

2. Greed-structure program;

3. Confident trading program;

4. "Have fun" program.

Although you use all of them in daily living and trading, you can use only one at any instance (they can be switched very rapidly, however). In this section, we will look at the four programs in the order of the size of the group of traders using them on an average day in the market.

Your own individual belief systems will determine what software programs you run while trading the market. A later section presents a methodology for manipulating your own belief system to improve your trading success.

To understand the market in terms of which software programs traders favor, we ran sample surveys of the trading population on both average and exceptional days. We found, for example, on an average trading day, 35 to 45 percent of the trading population were running their self-preservation program, 25 to 35 percent were running their greed program, 15 to 25 percent were running their confidence program and 5 to 15 percent were running their have fun program. Let's examine these programs individually and apply them to our own trading plan.

As noted in the previous chapter, the world is a mirror that tells us exactly which part of our brain we are using at the present moment. We, in turn, by everything we do and say, tell the world which software program we are running. Let's look at each program, starting with the largest group of traders on an average day and working our way down to the smallest group. In taking this route, we are starting with the largest group of losers and working our way to the winners. Remember that most of us switch quickly from one program to another and another, depending on developments, and that whatever program we are running at the moment determines our behavior and how we will present ourselves to the world and the market.

Self-Preservation (Fear) Program

On an average day, this is the largest group (35–45%) of traders in the market. The big mover within this group is *fear.* As fear traders, we demonstrate our concern with fear in everything we do or say. Whenever fear comes into our life, it propels us into the left hemisphere (our own in-house idiot), and our primary concern becomes protection.

The first physical signs of fear trading are: we start collapsing in the upper chest area, and we start to slump forward. We are then in a poor position for trading: 44 percent of all our oxygen normally goes to the brain, and at just the time we need it (a perceived crisis), we are cutting it off. Why? The entire organism senses crisis, and our body responds by starting toward a protective fetal position. Everything is done for protection, not profit. Our basic decision-making process is shut down in favor of frozen protectionism. If you are in a losing trade and you find it difficult to get out, it is because you are running the fear program.

239

In this state, you will overlook opportunities for getting in and out and making a profit. This program resists any change, including getting out of a losing trade. The program has its valid purpose, but it certainly does not belong in the *act* of trading.

This is, by far, the most *consistent* of the four programs. Its drawback is you almost always buy the top and sell the bottom—not a profitable strategy. I recommend keeping a diary of your trades and recording your feelings whenever you have a series of losses. From your diary, you can determine which part of your brain was being used when you initiated that losing trade. You will find that, most often, you were running this fear program.

In the methodology section, we will develop a procedure that makes use of this software's strengths to enhance rather than detract from our trading results.

Greed-Structure Program

On an average day in the market, about 25 to 35 percent of all traders are running a greed program and seeing the world through masses of dollar signs. A typical greed-structure comment might go like this: "Say, that is a nice shirt you have on, how much did that set you back? If you ever need more of that kind, let me know. I know where you can get them wholesale."

While running this software, we are more interested in price than value. When the market moves, we know exactly what it is costing us or exactly how much we are making. This program makes us suckers for "get rich quick" schemes, and we'll buy underwater lots in Florida and $3,000 black box trading software. We are sucked in by computer backtesting and optimization. That is the bad side of this software.

On the good side, this software is the best for discovering the *structure* of the market. It is the best for seeing the Elliott wave, Fibonacci retracements, technical formations, and so on.

This is not good software to run while looking at the monitors. Its purpose, like the fear program, is in analyzing and *getting ready* to trade the markets.

Confident Trading Program

On an average trading day, about 15 to 25 percent of traders are running the confident trading program. They can be recognized by the air of assurance they have about making money and being in the market. Here are some behavioral indicators that we are running this program: We want to make sure that everything is "appropriate." We say the right things, follow the right system, listen to the right advisers, wear the right clothes.

Users of this program tend to be name droppers and chronic interrupters. They communicate an urgent wish that you would finish telling your story because theirs is even better.

The important characteristic of running this program is that it exudes calm and sureness. There is little or no fear, and none of the damaging consequences of running the fear program. This is a noneffort program. You don't struggle to feel confident; in fact, if you struggle, you really can't feel confident.

Although this is a great program to use for trading, it isn't good for analysis. While running this program, we are literally "sharper and more intelligent" than when running any other program. We remember better and act faster.

At this level, we are beginning to use our core and our right hemisphere. The next program make even better use of those superstars.

"Have Fun" Program

This last and smallest group of traders (5–15%) are by far the most successful and happiest traders in the market! When you are running this program, you are interested in three things:

1. Sexual attractiveness;

2. Future promise;

3. New adventure.

These are the first traders to get into any new trend. This is absolutely the best program to consciously run while in the market. Like the confidence program, it is better at trading than at analysis. It is the opposite of the fear program: it is light, easy, and fun-loving. It creates a good time no matter what the situation. In this program, it is easy to change an opinion or a position in the market. Stopping and reversing are no problem at all. In the fear program, stopping and reversing are almost impossible. Where the "fear" program sees itself doing battle with the market, the "have fun" program sees itself being supported by and in sync with the market.

INTEGRATING YOUR PERSONAL SOFTWARE PROGRAMS

Let me emphasize that I believe these next few pages are the most important pages in this entire book. Please spend some time understanding (controlling) and practicing this process. It is lethal to losses. Take this advice with you every day in the market:

IN A NO-RISK
STRUCTURE
I CAN
HAVE FUN AND "HAVE FUNDS"

Through the years, working with our own personal trading and with thousands of full-time traders, we have developed a technique that will ensure that you can trade at Level Four and Level Five. As stated above, you have four different software programs and you can run only one at a time. You can, however, switch from one to the other quite rapidly. Each has its own unique capabilities, and we want to make full use of *all* of them. We need all the help we can get in trading the markets.

In a No-Risk

This segment means using the fear program to make whatever trading decisions fit into a maximum profit–minimum risk structure. Here is how you do it. First, use it outside the market trading hours, either the night before or early in the morning, before the market opens. Simulate a catastrophic day in the market. You know your present positions and, from using the Profitunity Trading Partner in Chapter 10, you already know where your stops are or should be. From your current positions, you can easily figure what your total loss would be if every position is stopped out. The dollar-and-cents amount is quite important to your planning.

Suppose your catastrophic stop-out figure is $6,500, which means that if everything is stopped out tomorrow, your account would be down by $6,500. If that does in fact happen, how will you feel tomorrow night while planning the *next* day's market activity? If your perspective will be upset and you will be too worried to sleep tomorrow night, your risk is too great. You must cut it down on the open by getting out of some of your current contracts. Let's say your pain limit is $4,000. Your task is clear: you must get out of $2,500 risk on the opening tomorrow.

Let me repeat, for emphasis: the most valuable commodity you will ever deal with is your perspective. Whatever else happens, you can't afford to lose that. A no-risk situation does not mean that you can't lose money. It is a psychological no-risk: you can't lose your perspective.

Structure

During this part of the analysis, you first want to determine your most likely position relative to the Elliott wave. Methods of doing this are explained in Chapter 7. Once you have determined your position in the Elliott wave, you then want to move up one significant time frame to determine your "air bag stop." Next, you determine what rhythms the market is in and then your exact entries and exits using the initiating and responsive fractals. If you decide to become even more aggressive, you can plan on trading the Profitunity windows and greens and squats. With a bit of practice, you should be able to analyze a completely new chart and know what your position should be on each bar, where to stop, where to double up, where to stop and reverse, and when not to trade—in less than 10 seconds. This technique will amaze you, especially if, like me, you have in the past spent hours each day on technical analysis.

Up to now you have been using your left hemisphere. At this point, your work is really over. Go out and have some fun. It actually is *imperative* that you stop working now. Go to bed, rest well, and don't think about the market. You are ready to trade tomorrow.

When tomorrow comes and you look at your screen, plug in the next line with confidence.

I Can

These two words represent the self-confidence you have because you know where you are and where the market is (via Elliott wave and fractals). Part of your confidence comes from your knowledge of structure. Besides, you know that you are in a no-risk position because you constructed your trading strategy to make this so. You are now trading from the core and the right hemisphere. There is no struggle, and the only thing left to do is to have fun trading. In fact, if you are not having fun, you are still in the left hemisphere and you shouldn't be trading.

Have Fun and "Have Funds"

Trading is much more like riding a bicycle or dancing than taking a math test. When you go dancing, you don't rush across to the floor to see how soon you can get there. You are there for the enjoyment and pleasure of living at that moment. If your confidence is built on understanding (controlling) the underlying structure of the market and yourself, you don't need to be greedy. The markets will be there tomorrow and next year and probably next century, if history is any judge.

APPLICATIONS TO OTHER SITUATIONS

If our premises about the market are valid, they should apply to other parts of our lives as well. And they do! For example, say you are coming to me for my help as a therapist. My very first task is to make sure that you feel in a no-risk situation. You must understand that there is a legally binding confidentiality about anything you might tell me. No matter what you do or say here, only you and I will know it. When you thoroughly understand that you are not taking any sort of risk being here, you begin to loosen up a bit. This relaxation may allow you to see parts of your life, and how you run them, in ways that have not been obvious before.

We must go further. We must set up some sort of structure in which each of us knows our role. I make the rules, but you are the leader. Wherever and in whatever direction you wish to move, I will support you there. My obligation is to share with you my thoughts and feedback about what is happening, without in any way threatening your safety and well-being. This structure must be crystal-clear and nonthreatening.

Once you realize that you are really safe and also understand the structure of the situation, an abiding confidence starts to build inside of you. You feel the power start to emerge from deep within. This building of confidence is automatic. Or, as described by one of my student traders, "It is really automagic, how it works!" It is important to note here that the confidence building is quite natural. It is not something you strive for or struggle to get. It *is* automagic.

After a while, another quite natural change starts to occur. You begin to have fun. Most new patients are not attracted toward therapy for the "fun" of it. Their tunnel tells them there must be tears and sobbing and boxes of tissues. Sometimes, this happens, but for very short spans. Our favorite tunnel includes a lot of laughter and fun times.

Everything I have said about the therapy process is applicable to trading and learning to trade. Most traders sweat, struggle, and shed tears over trying to become a trader when a better course is simply to enjoy being a trader.

It is all so simple—not necessarily easy, but simple. I guarantee it.

I once saw a bumper sticker that gave this advice: "If sex is a pain in the a_____, you are doing it all wrong." Permit me to bastardize the advice by saying: "If trading is not fun, you are doing it all wrong!"

SOME FINAL THOUGHTS

For freedom, security, having anything you want, and just plain having one helluva good time, nothing comes close to trading. The only thing comparable to the fun we have as a family is our private training of over 450 individuals who are now successful full-time traders.

The oldest was a fine gentleman of almost 90 years, who had the mind of a teenager. The youngest was a teenager who had the wisdom of a mature man. This youngest trader, whose name is Chip, had graduated from college at a very early age, traveled around the world twice on his own, and was recommended by a friend because of his spirit and brilliance. I hesitated a long while and insisted on meeting him several times before I would agree to train him. He was turned down by a quote retrieval service because the head of this worldwide company felt no one that young should be trading commodities.

He now trades from his house on a private island in the Gulf of Mexico with nothing but miles of beaches on each side and with no humans in sight. He uses a power generator, a satellite dish, and a cellular phone to trade. When he gets bored, he takes off on another trip. While finishing this manuscript, I received a letter he had sent from New Zealand. He thanked me for presenting this opportunity to run his life just the way he chose. I quote here only the last line of the letter:

> . . . This [trading] is the most fun I have ever had in my life, with my clothes on.

Go get 'em, Chip!

CONCLUSION

The theme of this book is that there are higher levels of consciousness to which we humans may aspire, and that those higher levels are infinitely more desirable than our present condition. This is the fundamental esoteric teaching, the one element that is common to hermetic and alchemical writings, the bhagavad-gita, the parables of Jesus, the teachings of the compassionate Buddha, the secret of the golden flower, Plato's

Republic, the enneads of Plotinus, Upanishads, and innumerable other sacred and secular texts.

Working toward these higher levels of being involves two complementary processes: first, the discovery that the goal—the higher level of consciousness—exists and is attainable; second, the actual attainment of the goal.

Two stories from the Bible illustrate these two states in the process. The first tells of a "treasure hidden in a field, which a man found and covered up; then in his joy he goes and sells all that he has and buys the field." The second is a story of "a merchant in search of fine pearls, who, on finding one pearl of great value, went and sold all that he had and bought it." In each of these stories, the initial discovery, the first stage, is followed by a second stage in which personal sacrifices are made and former beliefs and attachments are abandoned, in order to realize a new possibility.

When one (trader or nontrader) begins to transcend one's current limits, the most striking change is a profound sense of unity, a sense that all things are more than interrelated; they are all one thing. Just as the different facets of a jewel are two-dimensional aspects of a single three-dimensional form, so the various objects and events that we experience (in the transcendence state) are different three-dimensional aspects of reality.

The sense of unity, even in the market, extends to the perception of time. Instead of perceiving a succession of different moments, and movements within those moments, a trader in this state perceives all as being identical and therefore as comprising one eternal movement/moment. Time no longer flows or passes; it seems to stand still. Events still occur in sequence, but they do not seem to take place "in time." The effect of this stoppage of time is a marked sensation of peace and stability. This was the message that Don Juan was trying to get to Castanada about "stopping the world." In short, the stoppage of time is not separate from the intense good feelings of transcendent experience, but is an integral part of that feeling—another aspect of an experience that is, above all, unitary. When all things are perceived as one thing, all places seem to be one place, all markets seem to be the same market, and the idea of different places/markets (which is an idea of three-dimensional space) is perceived as illusion.

It is only in appearance that time is a river. It is rather a vast landscape and it is the eye of the beholder that moves.

Thornton Wilder
Eighth Day

Bibliography

Abraham, R. H., and Shaw, C. D., *Dynamics: The Geometry of Behavior. Part One—Periodic Behavior; Part Two—Global Behavior.* Santa Cruz, CA: Aerial Press, 1982.

Anderson, P. W., Arrow, K. J., and Pines, D. *The Economy as a Complex Evolving System.* Reading, MA: Addison-Wesley, 1988.

Babcock, B. *Trading Systems.* Homewood, IL: Dow Jones Irwin, 1989.

Bai-Lin, H. *Chaos.* Singapore: World Scientific, 1984.

Bak, P., and Chen, K. "Self-Organized Criticality," *Scientific American,* Vol. 264 (January 1991): pp. 34, 35.

Balan, R. *Elliott Wave Principle Applied to the Foreign Exchange Markets.* London: BBS Publications, Ltd., 1989.

Barnsley, M. *Fractals Everywhere.* San Diego, CA: Academic Press, 1988.

Beltrami, E. *Mathematics for Dynamic Modeling.* Boston: Academic Press, 1987.

Bernstein, J. *Timing Signals in the Futures Market.* Chicago: Probus Publishing Co., 1991.

Bernstein, P. *Capital Ideas: The Improbable Origins of Modern Wall Street.* New York: Free Press, 1992.

Black, F., and Scholes, M. "The Pricing of Options and Corporate Liabilities," *Journal of Political Economy* (May/June 1973).

Briggs, J., and Peat, F. D. *Turbulent Mirror.* New York: Harper & Row, 1989.

Brock, W., Hsieh, D., and LeBaron, B. *Nonlinear Dynamics, Chaos, and Instability: Statistical Theory and Economic Evidence.* Cambridge, MA: MIT Press, 1991.

Callen, E., Sculley, M., and Shapero, D. "Imitation Theory— The Study of Cooperative Social Phenomena," in *Collective Phenomena and the Application of Physics to Other Fields of Science,* ed. N. Chigier and E. Stern. Fayetteville, NY: Brian Research Publications, 1975.

Callen, E., and Shapero, D. "A Theory of Social Imitation," *Physics Today* (July 1974).

Casadagli, M. "Chaos and Deterministic versus Stochastic Non-linear Modeling," *Journal of the Royal Statistical Society* 54 (1991).

Chen, B., and Tong, H. "On Consistent Non-parametric Order Determination and Chaos," *Journal of the Royal Statistical Society* 54 (1992).

Chorafas, D. N. *Chaos Theory in the Financial Markets.* Chicago, IL: Probus Publishing Co., 1994.

Colby, R. W., and Meyers, T. A. *The Encyclopedia of Technical Market Indicators.* Homewood, IL: Business One Irwin, 1988.

Cootner, P., ed. *The Random Character of Stock Market Prices.* Cambridge, MA: MIT Press, 1964.

Dalton, J. F., Jones, E. T., and Dalton, R. B. *Mind over Markets.* Chicago: Probus Publishing Co., 1990.

Davis, L. *Handbook of Genetic Algorithms.* New York: Van Nostrand Reinhold, 1991.

Day, R. H. "The Emergence of Chaos from Classical Economic Growth," *Quarterly Journal of Economics* 98 (1983).

Deboeck, G. J. *Trading on the Edge.* New York: John Wiley & Sons, 1994.

DeGooijer, J. G. "Testing Non-linearities in World Stock Market Prices," *Economics Letters* 31 (1989).

DeMark, T. R. *The New Science of Technical Analysis.* New York: John Wiley & Sons, 1994.

DeVaney, R. L. *An Introduction to Chaotic Dynamical Systems.* Menlo Park, CA: Addison-Wesley, 1989.

Douglas, M. *The Disciplined Trader: Developing Winning Attitudes.* New York: Institute of Finance, 1990.

Dreyfuss, H. L., and Dreyfuss, S. E., *Mind over Machine.* New York: Free Press, 1986.

Edmondson, A. C. *A Fuller Explanation.* New York: Springer-Verlag, 1986.

Edwards, R. D., and McGee, J. *Technical Analysis of Stock Trends,* rev. 5th ed. New York: John McGee, Inc.

Farmer, J. D. "Chaotic Attractors of an Infinite-Dimensional Dynamic System," *Physica* 4D (1982): 336–393.

Farmer, J. D., and Sidorowich, J. J. "Exploiting Chaos to Predict the Future and Reduce Noise," *Evolution, Learning and Cognition,* ed. Y. C. Lee. London: World Scientific Press, 1988.

Feder, J. *Fractals.* New York: Plenum Press, 1988.

Fischer, K. L. *The Wall Street Waltz.* Chicago: Contemporary Books, 1987.

Flandarin, P. "On the Spectrum of Fractional Brownian Motions," *IEEE Transactions on Information Theory* 35 (1989).

Fritz, R. *The Path of Least Resistance.* New York: Fawcett Columbine, 1989.

Frost, A. J., and Prechter, R. *Elliott Wave Principle.* Gainesville, GA: New Classics Library, 1978.

Gallacher, W. *Winner Takes All.* Chicago: Midway Publications, 1983.

Gallway, T. *The Inner Game of Tennis.* New York: Random, 1981.

Gardner, M. "White and Brown Music, Fractal Curves and 1/f Fluctuations," *Scientific American* 238 (1978).

Garfield, C. *Peak Performers.* New York: Avon Books, 1986.

Glass, L., and Mackey, M. C. *From Clocks to Chaos.* Princeton, NJ: Princeton University Press, 1988.

Gleick, J. *Chaos: The Making of a New Science.* New York: Viking Press, 1987.

Graham, B., and Dodd, D. L. *Security Analysis.* New York: McGraw-Hill, 1934.

Henon, M. "A Two-dimensional Mapping with a Strange Attractor," *Communications in Mathematical Physics* 50 (1976).

Hofstadter, D. R. "Mathematical Chaos and Strange Attractors," in *Metamagical Themas.* New York: Bantam Books, 1985.

Jensen, R. V., and Urban, R. "Chaotic Price Behavior in a Non-Linear Cobweb Model," *Economics Letters* 15 (1984).

Jung, C. G. *Cenenary Brochure.* Zurich: Curatorum of C. G. Jung Institute, 1975.

Kasko, B. *Neural Networks and Fuzzy Systems.* Englewood Cliffs, NJ: Prentice-Hall, 1992.

Kaufman, P. J. *The New Commodity Trading Systems and Methods.* New York: John Wiley & Sons, 1987.

Kelsey, D. "The Economics of Chaos and the Chaos of Economics," *Oxford Economic Papers* 40 (1988).

Kilpatrick, A. *Warren Buffett, The Good Guy of Wall Street.* New York: Donald I. Fine, Inc., 1992.

Kindelberger, C. P. *Manias, Panics and Crashes.* New York: Basic Books, 1978.

Korsan, R. J. "Fractals and Time Series Analysis." *Mathematics Journal* 3 (1993).

Koza, J. *Genetic Programing.* Cambridge, MA: MIT Press, 1993.

Laing, R. "Efficient Chaos Or, Things They Never Taught in Business School." *Barron's*, July 29, 1991, p. 12.

Larrain, M. "Empirical Tests of Chaotic Behavior in a Nonlinear Interest Rate Model." *The Financial Analyst Journal* Vol. 47 (Sept./Oct. 1991): p. 78.

LeBaron, B. "Empirical Evidence for Nonlinearities and Chaos in Economic Time Series: A Summary of Recent Results,"

University of Wisconsin, Social Systems Research Institute, 9117, 1991.

Lebon, G. *The Crowd*. Delaware: Cherokee Publishing, 1982.

Lewin, R. *Complexity, Life at the Edge of Chaos*. New York: Macmillan, 1992.

Lorenz, H. *Nonlinear Dynamical Economics and Chaotic Motion*. Berlin: Springer-Verlag, 1989.

Mackay, C. *Extraordinary Popular Delusions and the Madness of Crowds*. New York: Crown, 1980.

Makridakis, S. S., Wheelwright, J. J. and McGee, V. E. *Forecasting: Methods and Applications*. New York: John Wiley & Sons, 1983.

Malkiel, B. *A Random Walk Down Wall Street*, 4th ed. New York: W. W. Norton, 1985.

Mandelbrot, B. "Forecasts of Future Prices, Unbiased Markets, and Martingale Models," *Journal of Business* 39 (1966).

Mandelbrot, B. *The Fractal Geometry of Nature*. New York: W. H. Freeman and Co., 1983.

Mandelbroth, B. "The Pareto–Levy Law and the Distribution of Income." *International Economic Review* 1 (1960).

Mandelbrot, B. "The Variation of Certain Speculative Prices." *Journal of Business* 36 (1963).

Mandelbrot, B. "The Variation of Some Other Speculative Prices." *Journal of Business* 39 (1966).

Mandelbrot, B. "When Can Price Be Arbitraged Efficiently? A Limit to the Validity of the Random Walk and Martingale Models." *Review of Economic Statistics* 53 (1971).

Miller, M. H. *Financial Innovations and Market Volatility*. Cambridge, England: Blackwell, 1991.

von Mises, Ludwig. *The Theory of Money and Credit*. Indianapolis: Liberty Classics, 1980.

Moon, F. C. *Chaotic and Fractal Dynamics*. New York: John Wiley & Sons, 1992.

Moon, F. C. *Chaotic Vibrations: An Introduction for Applied Scientists and Engineers*. New York: John Wiley & Sons, 1992.

Moon, F. C., and Li, G. X. "The Fractal Dimension of the Two-Well Potential Strange Attractor." *Physica* 17D (1985): 99–108.

Murphy, J. J. *Technical Analysis of the Futures Markets, A Comprehensive Guide to Trading Methods and Applications.* New York: Institute of Finance, 1986.

Naisbitt, J. *Megatrends.* New York: Warner Books, 1982.

Naisbitt, J., and Aburndene, P. *Megatrends 2000.* New York: Avon Books, 1990.

Neil, H. *The Art of Contrary Thinking.* Caldwell, ID: Caxton Printers, 1980.

Pacelli, A. P. *The Speculator's Edge.* New York: John Wiley & Sons, 1989.

Pardo, R. *Design, Testing and Optimization of Trading Systems.* New York: John Wiley & Sons, 1992.

Peters, E. *Chaos and Order in the Capital Markets: A New View of Cycles, Prices and Market Volatility.* New York: John Wiley & Sons, 1991.

Peters, E. "A Chaotic Attractor for the S&P 500," *Financial Analysis Journal* (March/April 1991).

Peters, E. *Fractal Market Analysis.* New York: John Wiley & Sons, 1994.

Peters, E. "Fractal Structure in the Capital Markets," *Financial Analysts Journal* (July–August, 1989).

Plummer, T. *Forecasting Financial Markets: Technical Analysis and the Dynamics of Price.* New York: John Wiley & Sons, 1991.

Plummer, T. *The Psychology of Technical Analysis.* Chicago, IL: Probus Publishing Co., 1993.

Priestly, M. B. *Nonlinear and Nonstationary Time Series Analysis.* New York: Academic Press, 1988.

Prigogine, I., and Nicolis, G. *Exploring Complexity.* New York: W. H. Freeman and Co., 1989.

Prigogine, I., and Stengers, I. *Order Out Of Chaos.* New York: Bantam Books, 1984.

Rosser, J. B., Jr. *From Catastrophe to Chaos: A General Theory of Economic Discontinuities.* Boston: Kluwer Academic Publishers, 1991.

Ruelle, D. *Chaotic Evolution and Strange Attractors.* Cambridge, England: Cambridge University Press, 1991.

Scheinkman, J. A., and LeBaron, B. "Nonlinear Dynamics and Stock Returns," *Journal of Business* 62 (1989).

Schiller, R. J. *Market Volatility.* Cambridge, MA: MIT Press, 1990.

Schroeder, M. *Fractals, Chaos, Power Laws.* New York: W. H. Freeman, 1991.

Schwager, J. *A Complete Guide to the Futures Markets.* New York: John Wiley & Sons, 1984.

Schwager, J. D. *Market Wizards.* New York: New York Institute of Finance, 1989.

Shannon, C. E., and Weaver, W. *The Mathematical Theory of Communication.* Urbana: University of Illinois, 1963.

Shaw, R. *The Dripping Faucet as a Model Chaotic System.* Santa Cruz, CA: Aerial Press, 1984.

Shiller, R. J. *Market Volatility.* Cambridge, MA: MIT Press, 1989.

Smith, A. *Powers of the Mind.* New York: Random House, 1975.

Steidlmayer, P. J., and Koy, K. *Markets and Market Logic.* Chicago: Porcupine Press, 1986.

Stetson, H. T. *Sunspots and Their Effects.* New York: McGraw-Hill, 1937.

Stewart, I. *Does God Play Dice? The Mathematics of Chaos.* Cambridge, MA: Blackwell, 1989.

Thompson, J. M. T., and Stewart, H. B. *Nonlinear Dynamics and Chaos.* New York: John Wiley & Sons, 1986.

Thurlow, B. *Rediscovering the Wheel: Contrary Thinking & Investment Strategy.* Burlington, VT: Fraser Publishing Co., 1981.

Tobias, A. *The Only Investment Guide You'll Ever Need,* rev. ed. Toronto: Bantam Books, 1986.

Tong, H. *Nonlinear Time Series: A Dynamical Systems Approach.* New York: Oxford Science Publications, 1990.

Vaga, T. "The Coherent Market Hypothesis." *Financial Analysts Journal* (Nov/Dec 1990).

Vaga, T. *Profiting from Chaos.* New York: McGraw-Hill, 1994.

Waldrop, M. M. *Complexity, The Emerging Science at the Edge of Order and Chaos.* New York: Simon & Schuster, 1992.

Wallach, P. "Wavelet Theory." *Scientific American* (January 1991).

Weiner, N. *Collected Works, Vol. 1,* ed. P. Masani. Cambridge, MA: MIT Press, 1976.

Wiggins, S. *Introduction to Applied Nonlinear Dynamical Systems and Chaos.* New York: Springer-Verlag, 1990.

William, F. E. *Technical Analysis of Stocks, Options & Futures: Advanced Trading Systems and Techniques.* Chicago: Probus Publishing Co., 1988.

Zeidenberg, M. *Neural Network Models in Artificial Intelligence.* New York: Ellis Horwood, 1990.

Zipf, G. K. *Human Behavior and the Principle of Least Effort.* Reading, MA: Addison-Wesley, 1949.

Zweig, M. *Winning on Wall Street.* New York: Warner Books, 1990.

About the Author

Bill M. Williams is the president of the Profitunity Trading Group and has been successfully trading since 1959. His main occupation is trading his own funds. He is also a consultant to foreign banks, producers, hedgers, and large traders worldwide.

His research over the past three decades has been on the cutting edge of applying advanced physics, mathematics, and psychological research to profitable trading. He has held workshops and seminars for over 20,000 traders and has privately trained over 450 people who are now full-time private traders. He has published numerous articles, has been featured on the front page of several of this country's largest newspapers, and has appeared regularly on national TV.

He is the developer of the Market Facilitation Index (MFI), which is now standard on many analytical computer programs worldwide, and is the discoverer of the fractal of the Elliott wave. He is the first trader to develop a practical and profitable use of the new science of chaos and is well known for his original 10-second complete analysis of any chart on any time frame.

He has produced a home study course, including manuals, study guides, audio and video tapes and computer learning disks, to help traders at any level maximize their profits.

He has received worldwide acclaim for his ability to turn losing and inconsistent traders into consistently profitable professionals. He still gives a limited number of private tutorials.

For more information, contact:

The Profitunity Trading Group
6100 Brandy Run Road South
Mobile, AL 36608-3338
U.S.A.
Tel: (334) 341-0292
Fax: (334) 341-0277

Index